ORDER FROM CHAOS

The Everyday Grind *of* Staying Organized
with Adult ADHD

by JACLYN PAUL

ORDER FROM CHAOS
The Everyday Grind of Staying Organized with Adult ADHD

Published by Summit to Sea, LLC
PO Box 65221
Baltimore, MD 21209

contact@adhdhomestead.net
www.ADHDhomestead.net

ISBN: 978-0-578-57887-3 (paperback ed.)
ASIN: B07B692G9N

First Edition, 2018

Just for the charm: 10 9 8 7 6 5 4 3 2 1

Please note that while all efforts were made by the author and publisher to provide accurate and useful information in this book, we cannot and do not promise any beneficial results to anyone who may use that information. Further, we accept no liability whatsoever for the use of or inability to use the advice and information presented. This book is in no way intended to substitute for consultation with a qualified health care professional.

Cover design by Nathalie Cone, www.nathaliecone.com
Graphics and print layout by Douglas Paul
Set in Adobe Minion Pro

For my family.

ACKNOWLEDGEMENTS

Thank you to Oli Stephano, my first writing buddy and (fittingly) the first backer for this book's Kickstarter campaign. And thank you to everyone else who backed the *Order from Chaos* Kickstarter, including Matt & Amanda Agnello, Kevin L. Crofts, Chris Paul, Amanda Oczkowski, Big T & Patsy G, Steven Allison, and Gina Pera. This early support convinced me I had an idea worth pursuing.

I owe much to my husband for supporting my writing every day. He also holds down the fort whenever I skip town for a multi-day writing retreat. As if I could ever forget, my grandmother calls me occasionally to remind me how lucky I am to have such a supportive partner, and how lucky modern dads are to be so involved in caring for their children.

I wouldn't have gotten where I am in life without my parents, who instilled responsibility and self-sufficiency in me from a young age. With each passing year, I discover new ways in which they have made me incredibly fortunate.

Faye and Anne, your editor's pen and keen beta reader's eye gave me the confidence to release this book into the world.

Lastly, if I finish a book, it's always thanks to the Red Pen Addicts Anonymous, who keep me writing and rewriting no matter what.

TABLE OF CONTENTS

INTRODUCTION

Imagine coming home from a long day at work. You walk in your front door, hang up your coat, and look around. What do you see?

Had you asked me that question before my diagnosis with attention deficit hyperactivity disorder (ADHD), before I began my organizing journey, I know how I would've answered: I see a mess. I see a coating of dust on the floors and the furniture. Hang up my coat? No way. The coat hooks are sitting on the end table. They've been there for the past year and a half, waiting to be installed. Piles of junk crowd the first five stairs leading to the second floor. I see a dining room table heaped with unopened mail. I know there's at least one overdue bill in there, but I can't bring myself to look. After I find a place to set down my bag, I walk to the kitchen and see a bin of unwashed dishes next to the sink — leftovers from a small party I had *weeks* ago.

Would you want to come home to this?

I didn't. I wanted a clean, tidy home. A place to retreat to after an exhausting day. A refuge. A place I felt comfortable — and proud — inviting friends and family. But I had no idea how to get there.

Keeping ourselves organized nourishes more than the façade we present to others. It lays the foundation for a satisfying life. To do what you want to do, to chase what you really want, to feel truly self-confident, you need to feel in control of your life.

Too many adults with ADHD have never known that feeling. We don't know what it feels like to finish a project on time (or at all) or feel proud of a job well done. When we read about traditional organize-your-life and personal development strategies, we feel left out. We assume they can't work for us. As our failures and our shame accumulate, we give up hope.

Of course, my mess extended beyond my physical surroundings. I suffered anxiety at work and feared being "found out" by colleagues who respected me. I forgot to pay bills on time. My employer's finance office asked why I'd failed to deposit checks they'd cut for me months earlier. I met any criticism from my husband with an explosive emotional reaction.

After a particularly damaging fight with my husband over the state of our home and finances, I began to seek change. I had first expressed suspicions of ADHD in high school. When my guidance counselor told me I'd need to ask my parents and teachers to fill out evaluations, I stopped pursuing it. At that time, academia — and my parents' home — provided enough structure and consequences to keep me in line. Now I could no longer strategize my way to an A.

My life was falling apart. Unsure where else I could turn, I reached out to my company's Employee Assistance Program (EAP). Many employers offer EAPs, which provide free, confidential short-term counseling and referrals for work and personal crises. I met with a counselor who assessed my situation and referred me back to my primary care doctor for a prescription.

From that day on, I worked hard to dig my way out of the mess. I kept learning about ADHD. I made an effective treatment plan (which included more than a simple prescription for stimulants). When the time came for me to quit my job to take care of my son full-time, this added a whole new challenge. I took primary responsibility for our household and created my own structure — my own day — every day.

And yet, even with this increased autonomy and responsibility, I managed to thrive. Our home isn't perfect, but it's always presentable enough for unexpected guests or impromptu dinner parties. I don't pay my bills late anymore. I end each week with an empty mail (and email!) inbox. I no longer feel like I'm wasting half my life looking for lost items or fretting about unfinished projects around the house. Against all odds, my life feels more peaceful and orderly than that of some of my non-ADHD friends.

Through those years of researching ADHD and interacting with the ADHD community, I realized how lucky my husband and I were. Two adults with ADHD (a fact we realized years after our vows), happily married, caring for a home and a small child, saving enough for retirement, enjoying a reasonable level of success in our personal and professional endeavors…it wasn't a story I heard often. Adults with ADHD experience nearly double the divorce rate of the general population[1]. Among couples who stay together, discord and financial struggles are common.

Eager to help others avoid the lessons I'd learned the hard way, I started my blog, *The ADHD Homestead*, in 2014. Since then, I've written over 100,000 words about my experiences building a satisfying life with adult ADHD. These words have reached tens of thousands of people around the world.

The responses from my readers inspired me to write this book. When blogging has felt most thankless, my spirits have been buoyed by people who take the time to say, "thank you." Or my favorite: "you've given me a lot to think about." Knowing my words had the power to help others — that they were helping others — pushed me to do more. To dig into my whole personal organizing journey, I needed more than an 800-word blog post, or even a series of them. I needed a book.

Think of this book as a quick-start guide to getting organized. I reference several popular organizing systems and tools and give you my take on how ADHD may have kept you from sticking with them. You'll learn how to mount a more successful attempt, and how to bounce back from failures and learn from them instead of seeing them as evidence that you'll never succeed. This is how you'll organize your life for the long haul.

As you read, you'll find my own story woven throughout. I'm sharing it with you for a few reasons. First of all, sometimes we need to laugh so we don't cry. I want you to know I've been there, and I still start to go there from time to time. My story shows you we're all in this together.

Most important, I want you to know you needn't feel ashamed. Never, ever let shame kill your motivation to get better. You deserve a good life as much as anyone, and you're capable of creating it for yourself. I hope you finish this book believing, if nothing else, that failures — even catastrophic ones — provide critical information we can't get any other way. The trick is to look outward when something doesn't work, not inward. Rather than "I suck," think, "what went wrong?"

And that's what this book is really about: succeeding at the daily grind of tending to our adult responsibilities while making room for a fulfilling life. Owning our unique brains

---

1   (ADDitude, 2018)

and our unique lives, and crafting a system that works for *us*. And reminding ourselves that giving up is not an option, especially if others depend on us to provide or care for them.

If I'd looked around the messy, dirty house I described earlier and given up — or let my husband give up on me, like he was about to do — imagine what my life would lack. I wouldn't have my family. I probably wouldn't have many social connections at all. I certainly wouldn't have started my blog or written this book.

I hope these pages help you get started on your path to a calmer, cleaner, more satisfying life. It's hard work — even harder if you live with ADHD — but it's worth it. Once you get going, you won't know how you lived any other way.

YOUR GUIDE TO THIS BOOK

Getting organized is a lifelong process. This isn't the only book you'll ever need, nor is this the only time you'll need it. You will fall off the wagon. I know I have, and I actually *like* doing this stuff. I can't promise you a perfect system. Life with ADHD tends toward chaos, leaving us in a near-constant state of course correction. From now on, you'll define yourself not by your success this week or next, but by how you manage to claw your way out of the chaos and back onto the organizing wagon.

I reference several other books, which I hope you'll read after you finish this one. My recommended reading chapter includes books about ADHD and books about organization. If you think ADHD is playing a leading role in your life, look up ADHD experts Gina Pera and Russell Barkley. Both have written excellent books about adult ADHD which will fill in any gaps I've left. Because this book is about getting organized, I provide only an overview of basic information about ADHD. There is much more to learn.

I've broken this book into a few core rules and principles. They build upon each other, so you'll get the most out of them if you read the book from beginning to end.

However, maybe that feels like a no-go right now. Let's say you're in the middle of an organizing crisis. You haven't seen the surface of your desk in months. You eat dinner surrounded by stacks of unopened mail on the dining room table. You feel like you spend hours every week searching frantically for lost items. Not only that, your house is so cluttered, you can't remember the last time you cleaned it properly. Now it's not only messy, it's downright dirty.

Maybe you don't want to admit to anyone how bad things have gotten, but you're dangling at the end of your rope and wondering what will happen when you finally lose it.

You can't wait three months to read a book and learn how to get organized. By then you'll have accrued more late fees on your bills, gotten into 87 more arguments with your spouse, and perhaps invited a rodent infestation into your messy kitchen.

Or maybe it's not like that. Maybe you just offered to host Thanksgiving dinner and it's only two weeks away. You need help now.

If this describes you, I hereby grant you a one-time pass. Skip ahead to *Rule #2: You Need a Container*, which begins with the chapter titled "Containment Before Control." *But come back as soon as you've calmed down a bit.* The preceding chapters contain a wealth of information about ADHD, how you've gotten to this point, and how you can up your chances of holding onto any successes you achieve this time around.

And now to recognize another individual who may be reading this book. Maybe you feel like a pretty organized person, but you know someone who isn't. This person lives in your home or otherwise operates in close proximity to your life. You have no idea why they can't get their act together, and you want to help them because they're driving you crazy.

I have you covered. Just please promise me you'll be respectful and kind and you won't do anything to make your friend or family member feel more frustrated. Trust me: it looks like we don't care, but deep down we're feeling downtrodden, embarrassed, anxious, guilty…all that messy stuff. It can make us prickly, and prone to retreating and giving up.

In this book I speak primarily to the person doing the work. I occasionally include a tip for readers helping a loved one get organized. If that's you, use these tips wisely, and with compassion.

That goes for all of you. We're all doing the best we can with what we have. Be kind to yourself. Be willing to forgive. Treat yourself like you would a friend who you very much want to succeed. Practically speaking, it's the best — and maybe the only — way to get where you want to go.

A SIDE NOTE ABOUT PRONOUNS

Despite inequality in diagnoses, ADHD is thought to affect men and women in roughly equal numbers. I talk about this on my blog, *The ADHD Homestead*. There is much to say on the subject, none of it related to getting organized.

For the purposes of this book, I use gender-neutral pronouns (they, them, their) wherever possible. Where a gender-neutral pronoun would compromise readability, I alternate between the male (him, his) and the female (she, her). All statements in this book can be applied to all genders.

WHO WE ARE VS. WHO THE WORLD SEES

"Lazy is as lazy does."

I scribbled these words onto the back of an envelope after yet another argument with my husband. It didn't matter that he'd said them. The words had power because I felt them. At 23, we were unbelievably young. We were new homeowners, newly married, new to sharing responsibility for our own household.

Neither of us had been diagnosed with ADHD…yet.

But was I lazy? I scrambled to record my husband's accusation — you'll notice, on a scrap of mail pulled from a pile somewhere — because I wanted to remember it. I wanted to hold it up against similar labels I'd received as a teenager: selfish, ungrateful, irresponsible, and yes, lazy.

When I looked inside myself, I saw someone different. I always had. Yet here I was: free from my family of origin and its labels, only to run up against them in my new life with my new husband.

Many adults with ADHD struggle with the dissonance between our true selves and the people we show the world. I've begged many times over the years, first of my parents, now of my husband: give me another chance. This isn't who I am. I'll change, I promise. Please let me show you.

In that argument so many years ago, my husband gave a familiar response: he was fed up with my mess and my excuses. It seemed awfully convenient that I had time for playing video games with friends but not opening three months' worth of mail. He wanted to tell me I was grounded, but he wasn't a parent and I wasn't a child. One thing was certain: he was finding it harder and harder to believe in me.

And do you know what? I couldn't blame him. Something had to give. After a lifetime trying to prove I wasn't selfish, lazy, or ungrateful, I was about to stop believing in myself.

THE REAL COSTS OF CHAOS

One day, I sat down and made a list of everything my chaos and disorganization were costing me. The list spanned the personal, professional, and financial.

- I lost money in every way possible: I misplaced checks and sometimes found them when they were too old to take to the bank. If I did find them in time, I missed out on the interest they could've made in my savings account. I paid late fees on bills, even though I had money in the bank — I'd just forgotten to pay them or lost the bill in my piles. I bought new items because they were on sale with a rebate, but forgot to mail the rebate form.

- I dealt with chronic health worries because I never scheduled doctor's appointments.

- I lived in constant fear of being "found out" by people who held me in high regard. I always felt others' trust in me was misplaced.

- I suffered from nonstop anxiety, waiting for the other shoe to drop.

- I struggled to create a social life in our new home. I either felt I didn't have time because I needed to catch up and calm some of the chaos, or I wasn't organized enough to make plans in the first place.

- I felt insecure in all my relationships, both personal and professional.

- I had nowhere to retreat. My life was such a mess, I had no space to gather my thoughts or be by myself. Chaos lurked everywhere.

- I rarely communicated with long-distance friends or family.

- I wanted to write a book and publish articles in magazines, yet dedicated almost no time to my creative pursuits.

All of these things left me feeling anxiety, panic, guilt, and dread every single day. I had no idea why my life was such a mess. I was a hard worker. Despite my outward appearances, I did care about my family, friends, career, and finances. Every time I got fed up with myself and cleaned up a little, I swore I would never let the chaos return. I had no idea why I failed every time.

Though it took me a couple more years to figure it out, the answer was ADHD.

ADHD: THE CHAOS MACHINE HIDING MY TRUE SELF

This isn't a book about ADHD. It's a book about getting organized when you have ADHD. But we ADHDers often find ourselves amid chaos because ADHD presents unique challenges to getting organized. The next few sections talk about those challenges and what they mean for ADHDers and people who cohabitate with us.

If you have no connection to ADHD and you're just here for the organizing goodness, you might want to skip ahead to *Let's Get Started: Find Your Why*. Of course, you're welcome to stick around if you're curious. You never know who you might discover secretly has ADHD!

At the beginning of my organizing journey, I wrote in my notebook:

> *I feel like there's an invisible force pulling me away from getting the laundry from the washer, putting another load in. What is that?*

That — the invisible force field between me and everything I knew I should be doing — was ADHD. But the term ADHD feels misleading. We don't suffer from a deficit of attention, but more an inability to corral it.

A little brain science: ADHD primarily affects our prefrontal cortex, the seat of our executive functions. This part of the brain controls what we pay attention to, how we respond, and what thoughts have the floor at any given time[2].

I knew my messy life was screwing up my marriage and my mental health. Yet I failed again and again to make lasting improvements. While adults with ADHD may want to be organized, calm, and reliable, consider these factors getting in our way[3]:

2　(McGonigal, 2012)
3　(Barkley, 2010)

- We get **uncontrollably distracted** by random thoughts and stuff happening around us (people chatting near our desk, remembering we were supposed to send Uncle Steve a birthday card, a spider building a web in the corner, you name it).

- We make **impulsive decisions** without thinking things through.

- We have **a lot of inertia.** Once we start an activity, we may have trouble stopping when we need to (even if that means dropping the ball on something important).

- We **don't read or listen to instructions** carefully (this makes paperwork especially arduous).

- We can have a **hard time completing tasks in the right order.**

- We **struggle to organize our behavior** and tasks in a way that makes sense.

Add that to the force field I described earlier, which usually surrounds chores we find unappealing. It's unsurprising so many of us live in a mess.

That distractibility and impulsivity lead to a host of other issues, too. My house was full of piles — unopened mail, half-emptied shopping bags, laundry, etc. — because I couldn't settle down and focus for long enough to figure out what to do with them. The only thing more overwhelming than the need for order was the difficulty of getting there.

THIS ISN'T ABOUT LOOKS, IT'S ABOUT EASING MY OWN SUFFERING

Bottom line: I was in a lot of pain, and I organized my life to ease that pain. I didn't do it because I wanted the tidiest house on the block or because I wanted my husband to stop hassling me about dirty dishes or late payments on bills. I didn't do it for anyone else. I did it for me.

Even though getting organized will improve every relationship in your life, the reasons for change must start with you. This is a lot of work. You can't get through it, and you definitely can't sustain it, based on a set of ideas from other people about what you should do or how you should live.

At the end of the day, you define what a good life means to you. And you'll get organized to create the conditions that make that life feel attainable. You won't create a good life from a feeling of obligation. ADHD doesn't work that way. This book will guide you on your journey to discover what *does* work, even if you have ADHD.

BEFORE WE PROCEED: A QUICK NOTE ABOUT ADHD

You don't need an ADHD diagnosis, or even a suspicion of one, to benefit from this book. However, I assume you picked it up because you've heard of ADHD.

Unfortunately, bookstore shelves, the Internet, and even the school PTA are full of rumors and misinformation. There are several excellent books available for those seeking more information about ADHD in adults, most notably Gina Pera's *Is It You, Me, or Adult ADD?* and Russell Barkley's *Taking Charge of Adult ADHD*. These books will give you a solid overview of what ADHD is and how it can affect your life and relationships.

For now, there are a few things you need to know before we proceed.

ADHD IS A NEUROBIOLOGICAL DISORDER, NOT A CHARACTER FLAW

Many people with ADHD have heard the common refrain, "This happens to everyone. You just have to power through it." It's true that everyone feels scattered sometimes. No one loves paying bills or doing housework. We all go through times of stress or fatigue where we feel less in control of ourselves.

So why can some people use ADHD as an excuse while the rest of the world just has to suck it up?

As ADHD expert Gina Pera writes on her blog, *ADHD Rollercoaster*[4], "People with ADHD are just like all other humans, only more so." Yes, ADHD symptoms sound like human traits — traits we all need to learn to reign in. But for people with ADHD, this may be impossible.

During times of significant stress, even the most put-together person may display ADHD-like symptoms. The key difference is context: the situation is finite and caused by external factors. True ADHD emerges in childhood and impairs our ability to function in multiple contexts (e.g., both at home and at work)[5]. While some cases of ADHD may be caused by brain injury, your genes are far more likely to blame. If one person in the family has it, someone else probably does, too[6].

All this to say, ADHD isn't your fault. You aren't selfish, reckless, or irresponsible by nature. Most people seem to have a double standard for chemical imbalances in the brain, as opposed to elsewhere in the body. One would not — we hope! — tell a person with Type I Diabetes to try harder because everyone's blood sugar gets out of whack sometimes. We'd expect this person to maintain their condition with insulin and a healthy diet so they could live a normal life. Why would we expect someone with a chemical imbalance in the brain to correct it by sheer force of will when we don't expect them to do it with their pancreas? The sooner you accept your ADHD as a part of your unique biology, not as a personal failing, the sooner you can begin to build a better life for yourself.

WHAT IS ADHD, ANYWAY?

For those still wondering what ADHD is, here's the briefest summary I can muster:

ADHD shows up in two areas of our brain function: *working memory* and *executive functioning*[7]. Working memory allows us to hold more than one thing in our brains at once. If you've ever run up the stairs, only to find yourself standing in your bedroom wondering what you came for, you've experienced a failure of working memory. Again, everyone experiences this from time to time. People with ADHD experience it nonstop, to the point where it impairs our ability to function normally.

---

4   (Pera, 2016)
5   (Hinshaw & Ellison, 2016)
6   (Barkley, 2010)
7   (Hinshaw & Ellison, 2016)

Working memory holds onto information until we're able to use it[8]. In addition to forgetting why we opened the refrigerator, having a leaky working memory means we lose information before our brains can move it to long-term storage. We forget a lot of things before we have a chance to act on them or write them down.

Our executive functions, on the other hand, give us the power to delay gratification, strategize, plan ahead, and identify and respond to others' feelings[9]. That's some list, isn't it? In the same way a diabetic's body cannot effectively regulate insulin, imagine your brain being unable to control these behaviors. This explains why ADHDers' behavior so often defies norms and expectations for their age group — and this persists throughout their lifespan, not just grade school.

ADHD isn't a gift. It isn't a sign of creativity or intelligence, nor is it a simple character flaw. And it's more than eccentric distractibility, forgetfulness, and impulsivity. ADHD is a far-reaching disorder that touches every aspect of our lives. If we leave it unchecked, it will generate chaos at home, at work, and everywhere in between.

---

8   (Hinshaw & Ellison, 2016)
9   (Hinshaw & Ellison, 2016)

WHY SHOULD I GET ORGANIZED?

A HOT MESS INSIDE AND OUT: THE SYMPTOM MANAGEMENT FEEDBACK LOOP

Our surroundings affect our cognitive abilities, and vice versa.

Years ago, I rearranged our two spare bedrooms to create a bright, orderly, inviting home office. I moved my desk out of a dark interior room of our rowhouse to a room with big windows and a southern exposure. This was a great move, except for one catch: I left the other room behind. Once I had the reward, I lost all motivation to clean up after myself.

This left-behind room became a dumping ground for everything we didn't feel like putting away: furniture, boxes, any junk you could imagine. Every time I went in there with the intention of cleaning it up, my thoughts scattered in every direction. The overwhelm paralyzed my brain. I shut the door without touching a thing.

It got so bad, I literally pretended this room did not exist in my house. The first time, it was for four months. I later abandoned it again, after gutting it down to the studs, for almost two years. But that's another story.

This four-month period of pretending I lived in a two-bedroom house while I paid a mortgage on a three-bedroom house hastened my progress to rock bottom. I was at loose ends back then, both personally and professionally. I hadn't gotten into the nitty-gritty of what my life was like with anyone, not even my closest friends. It was too painful to discuss.

Finally, I admitted I needed help. I feared I would never use the spare room again, and that was only the tip of the iceberg. When I spilled the beans to my doctor, she wrote me a prescription for a popular stimulant medication. With considerable trepidation, I took my first dose and opened the door to the Lost Room. By then it belonged on an episode of *Clean House* or *Hoarders*.

Internally, everything went quiet. For the first time, my frantic need to do 10 things at once just melted away — and with it, the head-spinning overwhelm that had chased me away from the Lost Room in the first place.

This time, I felt okay when I opened the door. I understood that some things needed to be thrown away, some put away, and others given away. Painfully simple. Obvious. Yet previously out of reach. After a couple hours, I'd sorted everything into bags for each destination.

Later, my husband came in to help untangle a huge ball of yarn. As I watched him work, I realized that in the past I would've been about to climb the walls. I would've gotten impatient, yelled at him for taking too long, tried to rush the process by grabbing the yarn, and eventually frustrated him enough that he'd walk out and leave me to work alone. Instead, I let him work uninterrupted.

By the end of the day, I had found enough misplaced cash to run to Target for a new rug and several picture frames to dress up the room. And the room was clean. A small miracle. Hope where I'd all but given up.

Did medication make this possible? Yes. Do I still take medication today? Yes. Does medication make life easy or allow me to take organizing shortcuts? Not one bit.

There's a difference between making things easy and making things possible. Too many people believe ADHD meds give us an unfair advantage or make it like we don't have ADHD. Sorry to disappoint, but no. As my husband puts it, "medication gives you a choice where you didn't have one before. You're still responsible for making the *right* choice." Meds make it possible to do the hard work of building a good life. They don't do the work for us, they only make the work as easy or hard as it is for everyone else.

I saw this clearly when my husband and I finally took the plunge and gut-remodeled our kitchen. "Major life disruption" barely scratches the surface of what we went through. Our kitchen, dining room, and part of the living room were out of commission for six weeks while contractors knocked down two full walls, took down a plaster ceiling, and built a new kitchen from scratch. Construction noise invaded through the floor of my office for more than eight hours every day. Workers interrupted me with questions. I cooked all our meals on a camp stove on the front porch and washed dishes in the bathtub. Clutter and dust landed everywhere. Displaced furniture and appliances from the kitchen and dining room had to move somewhere in the meantime. Our cabinets were delivered before the room was ready, and the boxes turned our entire downstairs into a rat maze. I tried to stay on top of my pieces of the puzzle: picking up backsplash tile, choosing appliances, writing checks, keeping drinks in a cooler for the workers.

In other words, this renovation was a time when a *neurotypical* person (for the purposes of this book, someone without ADHD) would've started to exhibit ADHD symptoms. The stress, interruptions, and disarray would've gotten to anyone. I started to feel like I was off my meds. I felt like a crappy friend, a lackluster writer, an impatient mom, and an unproductive human. One afternoon, I was outside and saw a kid I did not know being mildly irresponsible with a stick. Instead of asking him nicely to stop what he was doing, I grabbed the stick and broke it into little pieces in front of him. I was stunned by my lack of impulse control. Living in my house was like living without ADHD meds.

Do these meds allow me to function like a reasonably normal person? You bet they do — under the right conditions. And that's where it gets fuzzy. Because while meds make those conditions possible, they don't allow me to sail through life. I still have to try. In other words, if I keep my house/office organized, exercise regularly, maintain a daily yoga practice, prioritize and guard my time, and eat a healthy diet, the meds fill in the missing piece of the puzzle. They prevent me from destroying all those good habits.

It's a delicate balance. Managing my ADHD symptoms has allowed me to build an organized life. At the same time, that organized life is a critical piece of my symptom management. Give me a chaotic environment and meds won't help, yet without them I'm powerless to tame the chaos.

SO IS IT THE CHICKEN FIRST, OR THE EGG?

This sounds like a catch-22, doesn't it? Don't worry, you'll get it. It's kind of like learning to drive a stick shift: you need to give it just enough gas and let the clutch out just so for the car to move. No one does it perfectly at first. In fact, when I have to teach someone to drive a manual transmission, I have them start with *just the clutch*. We sit on a perfectly flat, smooth spot, and I give an instruction everyone thinks is crazy: let the clutch out without touching the gas. You have to do it slowly. Really slowly. You have to pay attention and back off if the car starts to shudder. But if you're gentle enough, something seemingly magical happens. The car starts inching forward. Not fast enough to get you anywhere, but it moves, and it doesn't stall. Once you get that, we talk about adding the gas.

And so it is with ADHD symptom management and getting your life in order. Obviously, you could never sit at a traffic light and practice easing off the clutch without giving the car any gas. You shouldn't even practice that on the road, ever, anywhere. But sitting in a parking lot, learning how the process is supposed to feel under your foot and in your body? That'll take you places.

To get and stay organized for the long haul, you need to keep your symptoms under control. For many of us, that means taking a stimulant medication *every day*. We don't just need our meds in effect during work or school hours. We need it at home, too. This will give you that feeling of the clutch under your foot. It'll inch the car forward. Think about my first dose of medication, and what it was like to watch my husband untangle a ball of yarn without screaming or wrenching the thing out of his hands. You need this baseline. From there, you can start the real work.

Eventually, you'll wonder how you lived any other way. But the first step is achieving the right feeling. Getting a glimpse of what it's like to have control over your brain and your behavior. Taking down that force field between you and the first step.

Will you stall out? A lot? Certainly. I've been driving for more than half my life, and I still stall my car on occasion. In the same way, I still lose control of my inbox and let piles accumulate on the dining room table. The goal is to learn what it feels like to drive without overthinking: for it all to come together, for you to get everything going just right, however briefly.

When you're putting your life in order, managing your symptoms — whatever that means to you — comes first. You cannot make progress with your ADHD running the show.

Lastly, some people feel uncomfortable with the idea of using stimulant medication to treat ADHD. Between stigma and misinformation about side effects, it's not surprising. Check the ADHD-specific books in the bibliography for more detailed information, but for starters, know this: stimulant medication isn't supposed to make you feel hyped up, drugged, lethargic, irritable, or anything else. If you have a bad experience, chances are you've encountered the wrong dose, wrong drug, or an inferior-quality generic. Fewer than 10 percent of people with ADHD fail to benefit from any of the medications currently available[10]. If at first you don't succeed, keep trying, even if that means finding a new doctor who specializes in ADHD.

---

10 (Barkley, 2010)

IF YOU'RE HELPING SOMEONE ELSE...

If you're under the same roof with someone whose ADHD symptoms are out of control, you know it's hard. This person may present a wholly different picture to the rest of the world. Prior to his ADHD diagnosis and treatment, my husband told me, "I don't have these problems with anyone else!" If he didn't have the same problems with others, everything had to be my fault, not his.

"Unless your ADHD partner also behaves problematically with your friends and extended family members," cautions ADHD expert Gina Pera in *Is It You, Me, or Adult ADD?*, "they might suspect you're exaggerating your partner's at-home behavior, and therefore offer little validation or support."

Well, I hear you. And let me tell you this: I know why you're nagging, I see you picking up slack, and I know you're just trying to survive. I've been there.

Hopefully this chapter has convinced you that you need to address the ADHD symptoms first. You have to know what it feels like to inch the car forward. Otherwise, you'll keep repeating the same failures, reinforcing negative labels, and sapping motivation to keep trying.

For some people, all it takes is some quality information on adult ADHD. If your ADHDer isn't much of a reader, offer to read passages from one of my recommended texts to them, or even buy the audiobook version. My husband changed his entire perception of himself after listening to *Is It You, Me, or Adult ADD*.

If they aren't there yet, Pera's book is a great resource for *you*. Written for spouses of people with ADHD, her book includes a full chapter on dealing with denial in an ADHD partner. The more you learn, the more you'll be able to break through.

Some of us are lucky enough to live in what I call a dual-ADHD relationship. I doubt my husband would've read a book about ADHD because I told him *he* had a problem. I slipped it in by asking him to read *Is It You, Me, or Adult ADD?* so he could understand *me* better. Once he started reading, he found more of himself than he expected. He came to me with a heartfelt apology and a promise to get himself evaluated for ADHD.

A FINAL NOTE: CANARIES IN THE COAL MINE

The systems I use to keep my life organized are pretty airtight. When they're working, they're working, and friends express envy at my super-organized state.

It's like driving the stick shift 99 percent of the time: starting smoothly, not stalling, not rolling back. You encounter hills and challenges, but thanks to muscle memory, you adjust.

What happens when you can't get the car to move?

I'm going to drop the car analogy soon, I promise, but not before I point out the most important takeaway here: this is a *system*. Managing your ADHD symptoms, getting organized, staying organized, it's all a system. Think of it like a machine. Machines break down. It's not always someone's fault. And when machines break, we fix them.

One day, my car's clutch pedal suddenly did nothing. I couldn't get the car into gear. I knew how to drive a stick shift. The problem wasn't me. Something just wasn't working. I got it repaired, and I was on my way.

I did not cry about how I always screwed up and I needed to try harder. I did not tell myself that everyone else could get their cars into gear just fine. I did not keep trying the same thing over and over, certain it would work this time.

I say this because it's easy to feel ashamed when you fail at a basic adult task like paying the cable bill, meeting a friend for coffee, or acknowledging that all the rooms in your house exist. It's easy to get personal, call yourself mean names, and throw in the towel. But you still have to fix it, just like you have to take the car to the mechanic.

My first experience with stimulant meds came while I was employed full-time. I did well on them until I got pregnant with my son and had to stop. I continued to do well, despite the fact that I now stayed home and had to enforce my own schedule and responsibilities. Pregnancy and breastfeeding raise estrogen levels in the body. My primary care doctor correctly predicted that this would provide natural relief for my ADHD.

After I stopped breastfeeding and went back on my meds, I noticed my systems falling apart. I swear by David Allen's Getting Things Done (GTD) system — I'm really obsessive about it — but I completely stopped doing my GTD Weekly Review. My inboxes overflowed. I could go an entire week without looking at my to-do list. Something was wrong.

The thing is, I knew I could do it. I knew I could hold it together with GTD just like I knew I could drive a stick shift. I knew what it felt like for things to be working correctly, and this was not even close. Like a helpless bystander, I was watching everything fall apart.

I could've told myself it happens to everyone, or I was still a new mom, or this was just my new life with mommy brain. But I knew better. I made an appointment with my doctor and told her what was going on. Being an ADHD blogger, I knew from writing previous articles that hormones can have a dramatic impact on ADHD symptoms, and on medications' efficacy. I asked to try a different medication and everything changed.

Once you experience success with a system, guard it carefully. Once you figure out what works for your life, family, and brain, don't let it go. When it breaks, fix it. And don't assume the problem is you. We ADHDers have spent our entire lives hearing "try harder," usually with some reference to what everyone else is doing. Forget that. Don't let shame lead you to believe every failure is personal.

Sometimes, a system fails because something else is wrong. My trusty Toyota didn't break because it sucked at being a car, and you haven't failed to get organized because you suck at being a person. But these failures give us clues: clues about our symptom management, or what kind of system will work for us. Shame, blame, and guilt obscure these clues. Try to let them go. When you do, you'll free yourself to troubleshoot and build that good life you've always wanted.

KEY TAKEAWAYS

- People with ADHD are not inherently selfish, lazy, or irresponsible. There are real, brain-based reasons why we struggle to align our intentions with our actions.

- If ADHD symptoms are out of control, organization will not be possible.

- Extreme disorganization can make ADHD symptoms worse.

- Medication won't fix everything, but it might reveal behavior choices where none existed before.

- Shame, guilt, and negative self-talk prevent us from learning from failures.

- Failures aren't personal. They indicate a problem that needs to be fixed, much like a car that has broken down.

MYTH BUSTING: HAVING ADHD MEANS I'LL NEVER BE ORGANIZED

"But [organizing strategies] don't work for me," my husband said. "That's what having ADHD *is*."

This was not a fun conversation. His perception is common among adults with ADHD and the people who love us: being disorganized is part of having ADHD. We can try, but strategies that work for neurotypical people don't work for us. At some point, pressuring us to keep trying is just insensitive.

Let me be completely honest: sometimes I *do* feel like having ADHD means I can't succeed, or I'll never be as successful as someone without ADHD. I think anyone with any disability feels this way sometimes. It can feel like I work twice as hard because I need to keep my ADHD under control. Getting to the starting line is its own project.

It's normal to feel discouraged sometimes. People with ADHD do have to work harder. I once had a friend tell me, "Most of the time, I just remember stuff, so I don't need to write it on my calendar." There is no medication in the world that will make this true for me. I write everything on my calendar: writing deadlines, birthdays, dental appointments, reminders to text a friend who's going through a rough time. Of course I occasionally wish this didn't require so much effort.

But there's a difference between difficult and impossible. Nothing will make ADHD go away. Even if you don't have ADHD, if you're reading this book, nothing will make organizing your life an effortless process. But there are things that will make it possible.

Despite what I said in the previous chapter about symptom management and how meds changed my life, meds don't make me a superstar at any and every organizational system. I still need to work with my brain. I've had to learn what works for me and what doesn't. Even if a friend swears by a specific app, cleaning schedule, visual filing system, etc., I know that if it doesn't feel right, I'm not going to use it well.

Many people can get by with a half-system. Many people can force themselves to get organized with a system they don't love or that doesn't mesh with their thinking style. People with ADHD cannot.

So, if you have ADHD (or if you're just naturally disorganized), are you doomed to fail? Maybe. If you think it's as simple as reading about one strategy and implementing it exactly as described, you're unlikely to succeed. But if you're willing to learn about your brain and what works for you, modify accordingly, and keep trying until you figure out what works, you're on the right track. If you're prepared to fail sometimes, even after finding the right solution for your life and your brain, and you're ready to climb back on the wagon without shame, then you're not doomed at all.

Bottom line: ADHD provides an explanation and a reason for a lot of things, but be very careful about using it as an excuse.

MYTH BUSTING: CREATIVE PEOPLE ARE MESSY! TOO MUCH ORDER AND STRUCTURE WILL STIFLE ME

My undergraduate degree is in fine arts. In art school, I noticed this weird commonality: artists are messy. My contemporaries often left their brushes out in the studio. They walked around with paint-stained pants. I remember meeting with a professor in her office, and every horizontal surface was stacked a foot deep with papers. When she looked for something in the piles, she had to be very careful not to trigger a landslide.

I didn't judge her. I chuckled with her while I helped shore up a teetering pile. Deep down, I envied her. She was a treasured mentor for me. I admired her creative work, her teaching, and her attitude. Somehow, she managed to live in this messy space without descending into madness.

Our society elevates creative messiness and the absent-minded professor. We view tidiness as a form of repression and conformity. We say we want to be more organized, but do we really?

We can all admit to envying a more-organized friend or colleague. But if you find yourself believing, deep down, that messy surroundings indicate right-brained creativity, you'll need to reckon with these beliefs before you can create an organized life for yourself.

Some creative people feel more inspired in a tidy space while some need a little more stuff around. Like everything, these preferences exist on a spectrum. However, we all deserve a space that supports and clears the way for our personal endeavors.

What that space looks like will vary from person to person. Let's all agree, though, that it ought to be:

- **Intentional.** Even if you don't want your space to feel sterile or sparse, it should look the way it does because of your conscious choices, not your defaults or avoidance.
- **Inspiring.** When you walk into your work or creative space, you should feel ready to get started.
- **Healthy.** Even if you don't want it too neat, you should be able to keep it clean enough that spending a lot of time there won't compromise your health.

IF YOU'RE HELPING SOMEONE ELSE...

Remember that stereotypes run deep. Your loved one could be maintaining a life of chaos not just because she doesn't feel capable of cleaning it up, but because she *fears* cleaning it up. If you're living with a messy right-brainer, talk about what it means to be creative. Learn about some creative people she admires, and what kinds of creative spaces they maintain.

Help her to recognize the conditions under which she is most creative. Does she do her best work surrounded by stuff, or removed from distraction? Is she wasting time and experiencing stress because she's constantly dealing with crises or trying to find misplaced items?

Approach the situation from a place of concern and respect for her creative time. Let her know you want to help her build a better environment for her personal pursuits. Remember that making character judgements about messy people may put her on the defensive not just for herself, but on behalf of those she most admires.

The bottom line is, we all exist on a spectrum. Many creative people may indeed enjoy being surrounded by stuff. But no one enjoys losing important documents, missing deadlines, or wasting precious time looking for lost items. These struggles are a drag on our inspiration, and we owe ourselves a space that nurtures our life and work. Though our tolerance for clutter may vary, our tolerance for disorder and disarray should not.

KEY TAKEAWAYS

- ADHD isn't an excuse for giving up.

- A messy life isn't a mark of superior creativity or intelligence.

- A messy person may resist cleaning up because they equate messiness with creativity and inspiration.

LET'S GET STARTED: FIND YOUR WHY

If you've been skimming the past few chapters because you're not here for the ADHD stuff, come on back to the table.

Throughout this book, I'll refer to your *Why*. Your Why is your purpose for organizing. It's the thing you'll come back to when you fall off the wagon.

Your Why belongs to you and you alone. That's why I'm calling it a Why, not a Should or a Need To. Your Why will not come from me or your spouse or your boss. It cannot come from anyone but you.

You see, motivation is tricky, especially for people with ADHD. At its most basic, we can define ADHD as a problem of self-control: that thing that enables us to do something other than our first inclination[11]. We've spent our life listening to people tell us to "just do it," even if "it" is something we really don't want to do. Everyone has to do things they don't want to do, don't they? But it's not so simple for people with ADHD.

---

11 (Barkley, 2010)

Take a small example: going to the gym. I've met people who do this — go to the gym and work out — so I can attest that they exist. I don't understand them, nor will I ever be one of them.

Yet I value physical fitness for a variety of reasons. It's part of my ADHD symptom management. Yoga is part of my personal spiritual practice. I need to stay strong and flexible for the variety of recreational activities (skiing, surfing, paddle boarding, biking) I engage in year-round. And yet I never work out. I can't make myself do it.

I am, however, in good shape. So far, I've spent my 30s being in the best shape of my life. In part, I set the bar low — a daily yoga practice can be as little as a single pose — and forgive myself readily when I lapse in my exercise habits. But I also remind myself, as frequently as I need to, why I do it in the first place. I enjoy running outside to get fresh air. When I go for a run before a long drive, I'm less likely to lose my temper with my family while we pack the car. I try to be extra mindful of my feelings during a good run. I imagine myself able to ski more difficult terrain because I've gotten my body ready.

Every time I slack off, I come back to my Why. I run, bike, and practice yoga because I want the confidence to feel good in my body. I want the thrill of advancing in a recreational sport I enjoy. I want the autonomy of being able to do work around the house without asking for help whenever I need to lift something heavy. I want the inspiration and focus I achieve in my work only after I take a morning jog. I want the freedom of running alone, outside, with nothing but my thoughts. I have never put on my running shoes because I *should* go for a run, or because I *need* to stay in shape. These reasons are not enough.

Likewise, I don't spend time every week clearing my desk and reviewing my open projects because I should. I don't empty my inbox to zero every day or two because I need to stay on top of it. I do these things because I value the security of knowing I'm not letting anyone down. I want the peace and confidence to spend the time writing a novel, guilt-free. I value reliability, and I want to view myself as a responsible person. Paying my bills on time and managing my money effectively provides the joy of being able to take a vacation or say yes to an adventure. Maintaining a welcoming home lets me accommodate unexpected visitors and schedule last-minute social plans without stressing about what the house looks like.

These are my Whys, and they are deeply connected to my personal identity. When I fail to serve these Whys, I stifle the person I feel I truly am — the person I want the rest of the world to know. I organize my life not because I should, but because it makes space for me to be my true self.

WRITING EXERCISE: WHO DO YOU WANT TO BE? WHERE DO YOU WANT TO GO?

If you're uncomfortable writing, try one of these alternatives for any of the writing exercises in this book:

- Sketch or doodle your ideas.
- Draw a flow chart.
- Record verbal responses using your phone's voice memo app.
- Talk to someone — a spouse, close friend, etc. — who will jot down your thoughts for you.
- Create a collage with pictures cut out of magazines or printed from the internet.

Let's start looking for your Why. Write your responses to the prompts below.

1. Take an inventory of what your mess and chaos are costing you. A promotion? Close friendships? Money? Mental health? Be specific. I summarized my inventory in the introduction to this book, and you're welcome to refer to it if you're having trouble getting started. Leave some space at the end in case you think of more later.

2. Just this once, indulge the labels. Pretend this list belongs to someone else. Jot down your impressions of that person. What would you assume about them, if you didn't know them?

3. Now, write down who YOU are, deep down. Write a list of characteristics that describe the person you know yourself to be. In what ways is disorganization preventing the world from seeing this person?

4. Write a list of things you want, but which the chaos has kept out of reach. They can be anything: a boat, more friends, a potluck dinner party, a new job. How do these desires connect with the person you wrote about in #3?

A NOTE ON REWARDS

I have this very clear memory from my teenage years of stealing off to my room with a big slice of chocolate cake. I sat it on my desk, got out my math homework, and told myself, "Okay. Every time I finish a math problem, I'll take one bite of this cake."

It wasn't the first time, or the last, that I used bribery this way. I've rewarded myself with food, a new living room set, and binge-watching television shows. In some cases, bribery works.

Bribery, however, comes externally. Long-term motivation is internal. Several years ago, I read a blog post by a friend with ADHD. He'd invented a motivational system called One Task, One Stone. He marked a mason jar with levels 1-12 and set a bowl of glass stones beside it. For every task he completed, he put one stone into the jar. As the jar filled with stones, he "leveled up" until he reached Level 12.

I loved this, and immediately adapted it to my task management system at the time. I tacked up a picture of a new couch and told myself, "When I reach Level 12, I will buy that couch."

It worked. I pushed myself hard, partly because I love having a goal, but I also hated the couch we had. When I shared my success — and recent furniture purchase — with my friend, he admitted he'd stopped doing One Task, One Stone. ADHD, right? I remained confident. Intent on continuing to level up, I started a new jar and set a new goal: purchasing a kayak.

I never got that kayak. The novelty of One Task, One Stone faded for me, just like it had for my friend. I stopped gaining new levels. While I'd been excited to work for the couch, proud to hit Level 12 and earn it, I couldn't sustain enough enthusiasm to repeat the process.

I know what you're thinking. *Rewards work! I bribe my kids all the time! I bribe myself all the time!*

Yes, rewards work. They work for initial habit formation or short-term projects. Remember the Lost Room? I rewarded myself with a new rug when I finished cleaning it. That helped me power through the project. But I can't buy myself a new rug as a reward for cleaning up the kitchen every night. That long-term commitment to completing a chore on a regular basis must come from someplace deeper.

In other words, go ahead and reward yourself for filing your taxes. Taxes suck, and they only come around once per year. Reward yourself for pulling the cardboard box collection out of your basement and taking it to the recycling center. But if you want to stay organized at a basic level every day, external rewards won't cut it. If they're anything like my rewards, they'll also leave you obese and broke if you overuse them. For the daily grind, you need a Why. And it has to be more than a new couch or a big slice of cake.

YOU WON'T JUST DO IT, OKAY?

If you take nothing else from this chapter, remember this: you won't *just do it*. Getting organized is not a matter of simply buckling down and trying harder. If you're currently unhappy with the level of disorganization in your life, take some time to figure out why that is — and what you're looking for. You need a reason for getting organized that will be its own reward. Something that will make you feel so good, you won't want to lose it, and even if you do, you'll fight to get it back. Humans, and especially humans with ADHD, need to feel compelled by something urgent and important.

"I should really catch up on my filing" won't lead you to long-term change. "I will treat myself to a movie on Saturday night if I get this filing done" may help you clear out your backlog, but it won't prevent that stack of papers from coming back six weeks later. Maintaining an organized life can be tedious. ADHD abhors tedium without purpose. Find your purpose, and you may have a shot at conquering measured doses of tedium.

KEY TAKEAWAYS

- People with ADHD can't force themselves to stay organized or complete undesirable tasks from a sense of obligation.

- Our work needs to be motivated by something urgent and important.

- Our most compelling motivation comes from our personal identities and desires, not from external pressures or rewards.

RULE #1:
YOU MUST MAKE PEACE WITH REALITY

DON'T SHOULD ALL OVER YOUR LIFE

How many things have you done because you think you should?

As newlyweds, my husband and I split time over Christmas and New Year's with our respective families. We spent a long time away from home, but we were young, and we still felt our parents' expectations to participate in long-held traditions. Then my parents' divorce added another stop to our holiday travels. For our son's first Christmas, when he was nine months old, we spent 12 days out of town: four days at my mom's house, four at my dad's, and four with my in-laws.

Because we should be fair, right? Our son's grandparents should be able to see their first grandson for his first Christmas. We shouldn't leave anyone out. We should, we should, we should.

But think about this from an organizing and ADHD perspective. Out-of-town travel, especially with a baby, requires significant coordination. I had to organize itineraries, packing checklists, and gifts. I maintained communications to plan three consecutive overnight stays. We had to prioritize well enough to fit everything — including a portable crib — into our car and leave room for gifts we'd receive along the way. It would've been an impressive feat for someone with no cognitive deficits, let alone two adults with ADHD.

After that Christmas, I announced the end of multiple overnights and extended time away over the holidays. Everyone would take turns. People would visit us for a change. And you know what? No one stopped speaking to us. No one even called to complain. And I started to look forward to Christmas for the first time in years.

When you try to get organized, remember it isn't all about skill and habit development. We must also get real about what's advisable, or even possible. Even the most organized person can take on too much. For someone with ADHD, that threshold may be lower than you think.

Doing things because we think we should, rather than because we must or because they serve our Why, leaves little time and energy for our true priorities. Be especially ruthless with activities that require a lot of your ADHD. Most people with ADHD struggle with tedious tasks like filing, paying bills, and reading and answering emails. Even membership in a social book club requires a host of skills that may not come easily: keeping track of dates on your calendar, remembering to get and read the book, checking in on the group's preferred communication channel, securing a babysitter if you'll need one, and organizing a contribution to any potluck food and drink the group might share when it meets. Add up enough of these just-for-fun commitments and you may find yourself in complete gridlock.

This gridlock creates stress for you and your family, and it makes you feel like you've failed — again. And not just at filing your tax return, which everyone hates and puts off until the last minute, but at something others seem to do with no effort at all. The no effort part is likely a façade, of course, but the hit to your self-esteem is quite real.

Don't be afraid to challenge assumptions and habits that "should" all over your self-confidence.

WRITING EXERCISE: WE ALL HAVE OUR SHOULD

Your should can be the enemy of your Why. Sit down in a quiet place. Make your own list of shoulds, using the examples that follow as inspiration. Where are you feeling pressure from others, or from your own expectations, to stretch yourself thin?

Should		Reality
We should upgrade to a house with more space and bigger closets.	vs.	Our current home should be adequate for our family, but we're struggling to keep it clean and organized. Excess storage and living space will only increase these responsibilities and set us up for more stress.
Our homeowners' association needs a secretary. I have the skillset — I should volunteer.	vs.	I'm already barely keeping my head above water with my own email and record-keeping. Adding more will subtract from time I can spend on our family.
We should see my mom more. She's always talking about how her friends' grandkids visit every month.	vs.	Traveling with ADHD can be stressful, before even adding the kids to the equation. The time we spend preparing and packing everyone up, not to mention the weekend away, eats into our family time and leaves no chance to catch up on anything around the house. Mom is retired and in good health. We need to talk to her about visiting us more often and make sure she feels welcome.
We should have credit cards with our favorite stores because they offer great deals and rewards.	vs.	People with ADHD generally dislike paperwork. Each new credit card brings its own set of up-keep responsibilities: paying and filing the bill each month, keeping an eye out for fraudulent transactions, handling the junk mail and email from these merchants, etc. Not only that, it's easy to justify extra spending when we get special coupons and discounts. These cards may not be worth the cost to our time or our bank account.
I should sign up for this e-newsletter. It's full of information about free online courses I'd love to take.	vs.	I have over 4,000 unread emails in my inbox right now. Half of them are various e-newsletters that will either distract me from something more important, or I'll never read them. The course information is available online. I'll look it up if I need it.

THE MANY SHOULDS OF MODERN PARENTING

Another biggie for my generation is balancing work and family. Women in previous generations fought for mothers to have a place in the workforce. We now enjoy extensive benefits and legal protections to ensure that having a family and having a career needn't be mutually exclusive.

Consequently, many women feel they should continue to work after having a baby. And the research shows that some of them are right. Children seem to thrive more not in one situation or another — in daycare versus at home with Mom — but when their parents are happy. In other words, a child of a mother who wants to work is probably better off if she does, rather than if she stays home out of a feeling of obligation.

But be careful. Some parents with ADHD may flounder as full-time caregivers, while others will suffer when asked to balance work and family. Liz, a mother with ADHD and the writer behind the blog *A Dose of Healthy Distraction*, writes, "I dreamed of having a baby and staying home."[12] And yet Liz "never quite settled into" life as a stay-at-home parent. Expectations became overwhelming, and she ended up feeling "like a rat in a maze."

I, too, planned to stay home with my son. Before he was born, I had a job managing human resources and IT support for a small non-profit. Quitting made financial sense. If I'd kept working, we barely would've broken even after taxes and childcare. Emotionally and cognitively, I couldn't imagine dealing with others' problems (professionally, of course) all day, fighting traffic to get to daycare, and squeezing everything I could out of the few hours at home before I went to bed. Before having a child, my husband and I had struggled to balance work with household responsibilities. After? I didn't want to find out.

In fact, I wanted to write a novel. I wanted to turn *The ADHD Homestead* into a helpful resource for managing home and family with ADHD. I knew, deep down, that I could not do these things while raising a child and working full-time. My life as a stay-at-home parent hasn't been easy, but I wouldn't have done it any other way.

Liz and I are both mothers with ADHD. I'm certain ADHD played a big role in each of our decisions, even though we ended up in opposite situations. Remember: ADHD symptoms exist on a spectrum, and people with ADHD are still individuals. As Liz writes, "Everyone has to make decisions based on what works for their family and personal situation." Don't get caught up in societal pressures or mommy wars. Get to know yourself and do what's right for you and your family — not what anyone else says you should.

---

12 (Lewis, 2017)

KNOW THYSELF

As we challenge ourselves on all those little shoulds, as we ask ourselves "why?", we come upon another reality: who we are informs how we ought to solve problems and organize our lives. Don't overlook the many small decisions you make every day — decisions that should be informed by your unique brain and your specific situation. The tools you use to organize your life can make or break your success.

For example, do you care if an app on your phone is ugly? My husband's job, where he has spent up to 20 consecutive hours working on his team's web app, is to create attractive user interfaces. A bad user experience feels to him like a poorly-written book feels to me: grating and intolerable.

As the resident IT expert at a previous job, my boss called me into her office to see a great new calendar and task app she'd discovered. When I looked at it, I was horrified. The app was so hideous, its color scheme so jarring, I couldn't focus on its features or content at all. But it was perfect for her. She didn't care about the aesthetics. She'd found an app with the feature set she needed.

Knowing which of these user types you align with most closely will help you narrow — or broaden — your search for the perfect organizing tool. If you're helping someone else get organized, it will be critical to learn about their brain and recommend solutions that align with their needs. What feels perfect for you may be unusable for them.

In the following pages, I'll introduce several ways of thinking about your behavior and tendencies. While it's a good idea not to get too caught up on types and generalizations, they can help you get to know yourself. I've found it both helpful and liberating to be able to classify my behavior traits and adapt my organizing strategies to suit my brain.

Some of these classifications have their roots in scientific research and have been adopted widely. Others have not. All will provide some insight and help you get to know yourself and your brain.

RUBIN'S '4 TENDENCIES'

When we talk about getting organized, we must look at who we are. Not just as people with ADHD, but as individuals with our own sources of intrinsic motivation. The first step is, of course, finding our Why. But beyond our Why lies a complex web of character traits that tell us a lot about which approaches are likely to succeed — and which will not.

"If we know ourselves," writes Gretchen Rubin in her book *Better Than Before: Mastering the Habits of Our Everyday Lives*, "we're able to manage ourselves better, and if we're trying to work with others, it helps to understand *them*." Otherwise, we're stuck trying to swim upstream: a feeling familiar to many people with ADHD, not to mention those who live with us.

At no point has this been clearer to me than when I had a conversation with my husband about lists. Since I was a teenager, I've used them to calm down. Overwhelmed? Make a list! Anxious about forgetting something? Put it on a list!

As a human resources manager, I instituted several checklists in my office: a coversheet for our employee files. A new hire intake checklist. A first-day-at-the-office checklist. I dreaded leaving a key document out of our HR files, forgetting to set up someone's desk with the proper gear on their first day, or neglecting to collect all the necessary information to add someone to our payroll. A list was the only way to prevent that dread. Lists also helped when my boss asked me about my progress on these tasks; I knew immediately what I'd done and what I had left to do.

My husband, on the other hand, is repelled by lists. He may feel excited to set up a new gadget for me after work, but the sparkle fades if I put it on a list of things to do. I was shocked to learn that the very fact that something is on a list significantly decreases his desire to complete the task. For someone who will often add an item to a list just for the satisfaction of checking it off, this was a revelation.

Part of this is, I'm sure, related to his desire to surprise and delight. Simply meeting expectations is boring. Seeing someone's eyes light up when you've surprised them with a special favor? Now that's something.

I also suspect my husband is what Rubin would call a *Rebel*. In *Better Than Before*, she defines four tendencies, and claims knowing our tendency will unlock the key to long-term habit formation and maintenance.

Read these descriptions of Rubin's Tendencies and see if one seems to fit you:

- *Upholders* are all about expectations, both internal and external. These are the people who will follow a rule just because. If it's on their schedule or list, they want to do it, even if it's not actually that important. I suspect more than one Upholder with ADHD has used this to corral their brain into accomplishing what needs to be done, but also driven a loved one crazy with their inflexibility.

- *Questioners* will follow any expectations, as long as they make sense. (To be fair to my husband, I think he's a Questioner leaning toward Rebel). They need to feel, deep down, that a rule or expectation is justified. Otherwise it feels arbitrary and pointless. They also have a maddening tendency to reject expert opinions in favor of their own research. Questioners with ADHD may be especially prone to hyperfocusing on a topic and refusing to listen to others' advice or direction.

- *Obligers* almost always satisfy external expectations, but fall short on inner ones. For those of us with ADHD, that often means putting ourselves under tremendous pressure not to let anyone else down, yet letting ourselves down every day. While an Obliger may have little trouble coming through for others, they struggle to self-motivate without external consequences.

- *Rebels* need choice and freedom. Asking or telling a Rebel to do something will often lead them in the other direction. This spells trouble for maintaining good habits or order, and seems to lean toward chaos. If Rebels maintain an organized life, it must be because they feel they are choosing to do so — every day. The Why is especially important for Rebels. Be careful not to automatically generalize people with ADHD as Rebels. A person with poorly managed ADHD may not be oppositional by nature. It's possible his brain has learned, subconsciously, to behave this way as a form of mental stimulation.

Though these tendencies aren't based in scientific research, such generalizations can be helpful when considering why we've failed to keep good habits and stay organized in the past. Imagine if I tried to motivate my husband in the same way I motivate or organize myself: by starting with a list. His motivation would tank right out of the gate!

DR. AMEN'S ADD SUBTYPES

I've reviewed Dr. Daniel Amen's popular book *Healing ADD* on my blog[13], and I refer to it often. Despite valid criticisms from the scientific community, Dr. Amen's seven ADD subtypes offer a helpful way to think about ADHD. Too frequently, people assume the disorder manifests similarly in everyone. That's not true. Even within our small household, my husband and I are two very different people — both of whom have ADHD.

In *Healing ADD*, Amen devotes a chapter to each of these subtypes. A brief description is also available on the Amen Clinic's website[14].

- People with *Classic ADD* are "inattentive, easily distracted, disorganized, impulsive, restless, and hyperactive." The harder they try to focus, the more their brains work against them.

- *Inattentive ADD* manifests similarly, but without the hyperactivity or impulsive behavior.

- People with *Overfocused ADD* struggle to shift gears. This can make them appear inattentive or lead them down rabbit holes. Overfocusers can also get stuck in negative thought or behavior loops. They're prone to obsessiveness and worry, and can be inflexible and argumentative.

- *Temporal Lobe ADD* includes the symptoms of Inattentive ADD, and may or may not include hyperactivity and impulsivity. However, these people have increased memory issues, a short fuse, and are prone to dark thoughts.

- Someone with *Limbic ADD* suffers from a combination of Inattentive ADD symptoms, combined with chronic depression. She tends to isolate herself, and her glass is always half-empty. She may or may not be hyperactive.

- *Ring of Fire ADD* combines many of the symptoms described above: Inattentive ADD, hyperactivity, oversensitivity, oppositional behavior, and cyclic moodiness.

- *Anxious ADD* leads someone with Inattentive ADD symptoms to feel constant anxiety and tension. He usually predicts the worst, and will freeze under pressure.

---

13   (Paul, 2015, May 4)
14   (Amen Clinics, 2017)

If your ADHD doesn't quite fit the stereotypical descriptions you've been hearing all your life, you may find Amen's *Healing ADD* an enlightening read. I always caution potential readers that Amen's subtypes haven't been adopted by other clinicians, nor has the effectiveness of the Amen Clinics' proprietary supplement blends been clinically proven. That said, Dr. Amen is deeply knowledgeable about ADHD, and his insights have helped a great many people.

Bottom line: your ADHD may not look like your son's ADHD, which may not look like your mother's ADHD. It runs in families, but ADHD manifests differently in each individual. What works for one person may not work for another.

LEARNING STYLES

As part of my high school curriculum, I took a learning styles assessment that stuck with me. It provided my first big insight into learning and cognitive differences, and what these mean for us as individuals. When I started a new job shortly thereafter, I made sure to tell my boss I learned best by doing and needed to start operating the cash register right away.

In college I met my husband, who possesses a brain wholly different from my own. While he absorbs and retains information better than I do, he consistently underperformed on tests. I know how to ace a test, but not always how to apply the knowledge later on. This struck me as terribly unfair, that school should be so much more difficult for him. Now, in our adult life, I try to remain sensitive to our unique strengths and weaknesses and structure our household accordingly.

When it comes to staying organized, it helps to know if you're a visual, auditory, or tactile thinker. Here's a summary of learning styles similar to the one I first encountered, courtesy of the Pennsylvania State Higher Education Assistance Agency (PSHEAA)[15]:

- *Auditory* folks learn by hearing and listening. They store information based on the way it sounds, and often find themselves reading out loud to understand a passage of text more completely. When an auditory learner begins to fidget, she often hums or talks to herself or others. Seeing something isn't sufficient to internalize it. An auditory learner needs to hear it, too.

- By contrast, *visual learners* can easily visualize what they're learning. They like to see pictures. Spoken instructions can be challenging, and a visual learner may be especially distracted by sounds. They're drawn to color, and to concepts and stories that are rich in imagery.

---

15 (Pennsylvania Higher Education Assistance Agency, 2017)

- A *tactile learner* takes in the world by touching and doing. These are the hands-on people who love to move, build, and draw. They struggle to sit still and require frequent breaks. You may be able to spot a tactile person by the way he gestures and talks with his hands. Computers can reinforce learning for tactile learners by engaging their sense of touch.

Curious about your learning style? PSHEAA offers a brief online quiz at their website: http://bit.ly/PSHEAAlearningstyles.

What does this school stuff have to do with staying organized? Well, our learning styles tell us something unique about our brains. When I took the PSHEAA online questionnaire, it told me I'm 60 percent auditory, 30 percent tactile, and 10 percent visual. Meanwhile, my husband's revealed he is 20 percent auditory, 40 percent tactile, and 40 percent visual.

He and I must cooperate to maintain order in our house, but we have very different needs. For example, I love to be thrifty and reduce waste. I reuse file folders until they're too worn to perform their duties. Finding a treasure trove of old, useless files in the basement, I immediately put them to use in our filing cabinet. These folders were all different colors. This didn't register at all with me because they were all file folders, and all labeled with their contents. They all felt the same to me as I ran my hand over them. However, to my husband, the colors had to *mean* something. That they didn't, and the file folders were a variety of colors with no rhyme or reason, made the filing cabinet unusable for him.

If you're living with another human, this is a relevant example. Visual thinkers will respond well to color coding, whereas auditory thinkers probably won't care. I organize my reference books in such a way that I can run my fingers over their alphabetized spines to find the right one (a tactile experience I cannot replicate with an eBook). An auditory person may be motivated by music or conversation during tedious organizing tasks, whereas a tactile individual will need to get up from time to time and move his body for a break. Extraneous sound may drive a visual thinker crazy when he's trying to concentrate.

As a person with ADHD, you should be especially sensitive to the conditions under which your brain functions best, and the types of distractions that will derail you the most. Don't try to power through a situation that isn't optimized for your brain. An organizational system built on tools you find unappealing or distracting will not succeed. Surround yourself with the most helpful tools and systems for your unique brain and you'll spend more energy maintaining order and calm in your life — and less trying to force a square peg into a round hole.

ARE YOU A MORNING PERSON OR A NIGHT OWL?

Researchers studying at-risk students, drop-outs, and truants have found an interesting thread: most are not morning people. When given the opportunity to learn at a time more conducive *for them* — e.g. late morning, afternoon, or evening — many of these students show marked increases in achievement[16].

Think about this. When do you do your best work? When do you find yourself most motivated? Most focused?

As a writer, I constantly hear from other writers, many of them also parents, who burn the midnight oil after their children go to bed. Others congregate via the Twitter hashtag #5amwritersclub to sneak in an hour or two of writing before the rest of the family wakes up.

While both of these activate my shoulds, I've had to reject the romantic vision of myself as a writer choosing my craft over sleep. Staring at a screen after 9:00 p.m. is a recipe for wasted time and effort, and I simply don't do my best creative work before the sun comes up. Sleep deprivation intensifies my ADHD symptoms beyond anything medication can mitigate. I'm just not that kind of writer.

I'm the kind of writer who shows up every day, but between the hours of 10:00 a.m. and 2:00 p.m. If I had a job outside my home office, I'd be a lunch break writer. And that's okay. As for getting organized, I think a great deal about which tasks I do best at each time of day:

- I save mindless tasks for the evening, when I can do them in front of the television after my son goes to bed.
- I do less demanding tasks first thing in the morning, before my meds have kicked in.
- I do my least appealing work at the beginning of the work day, before I'm tired, and before my coffee and meds start to fade.
- I avoid doing anything on the computer after 9:00 p.m., and don't plan anything too mentally demanding for after-dinner hours.
- I never, ever pull all-nighters.

If the writing community is any indication, plenty of people work well at very early and late hours of the day. I don't. If you don't either, honor that. Figure out what time of day each kind of task — physically moving stuff around and tidying up, sitting at a desk and paying bills, sorting and filing paperwork, discussing plans with your spouse, etc. — comes most

---

16 (Dunn, 2002)

easily to you. Accommodate these tendencies in your schedule whenever you can. Your brain, and probably your family, will thank you.

KEY TAKEAWAYS

- People with ADHD are individuals on a spectrum. What works well for one person may not work at all for another.

- Time of day, color of the folders in a filing cabinet, and even the type of light bulbs in your office can affect productivity. Honor this and try to create a supportive environment.

- We all have different personalities, tendencies, learning styles, and ADHD symptoms. Learning about these differences and tailoring our lives to suit will increase chances of success.

GET REAL

The bottom line for *Rule #1* is, don't sweat what everyone else is doing. Do your thing. Make sure you figure out what your thing is first, but then don't let anyone steer you wrong.

Read this story from the early years of my marriage and think about how much time I spent dealing with out-of-control projects rather than facing reality and getting myself organized.

FOLLOWING IN OUR PARENTS' FOOTSTEPS

When my husband and I first married, we bought the old rowhouse where we still live today. The kitchen and upstairs bathroom both needed an overhaul, and the basement was only partially finished. Old houses also just require constant love and care. Our home was move-in ready, but with a list of future projects.

My husband thought he wanted to complete these projects. His parents had purchased a fixer-upper as newlyweds, then sold it for a handy profit shortly after he was born. He saw this as a crucial rung in their success ladder, and he was eager to replicate it. It sounded very romantic: coming home from work and spending hours working on the house. Using our sweat and skills to do for very little money what would cost others a small fortune. Watching that work turn into something that would catapult us to a prosperous life.

Maybe it sounded romantic. I agreed to all of it because I love working with my hands. My first job was in a cabinetry shop. I'm the type of ADHDer who's happiest when doing hard labor.

Nine years later, we had redone neither kitchen, nor bathroom, nor basement. We had remodeled one bedroom, which had sat stripped down to the bare studs for nearly two years.

We spent those nine years putting down roots that would make it hard to leave the house and its projects behind for something more practical. I fell in love with the neighborhood. Our son was born, and he joined a group of children who play outside together on almost every nice day. The housing market crashed, then rebounded with gusto. But as the seller's market returned, I didn't want to sell.

I wanted to pay for a new kitchen, and I did. The kitchen is beautiful. That I did not build it myself doesn't bother me a bit. At long last, my husband admitted it: he didn't love doing that work. It wasn't how he wanted to spend his time. He wanted the end result, and he was happy to pay for quality work rather than do it himself.

But for almost a decade, he'd clung to that idea that his parents had done it right. And they *had* done it right — for them. Working on the house together is just not our thing, and that's okay. Remember what I said about shoulds? Whether we admire our parents and want to emulate them, or we want to avoid making the same mistakes they did, a lot of our shoulds come from our families.

People with ADHD hear a lot from other people about what we should do. We hear a lot of labels, a lot of lectures, and a lot of advice. It's hard to move past all that and figure out who we are as individuals. Sometimes we look at a successful older sibling and feel the weight of expectations to do exactly what they did. But if it's not right for us, we're never going to feel successful.

In our family, doing every home improvement project ourselves is not right for us. That doesn't make us incapable or lazy. It does make us the people who knocked down all the plaster in our spare bedroom, then left it that way for a year and a half. It does make us the people who lived with a kitchen the size of a closet for almost a decade. But those things happened because we were not being true to ourselves.

Projects get out of control when we expect something from ourselves that we cannot provide. Go back to your Why. That is what will give you ultimate satisfaction and drive you to do what you need to do. Not what your parents did, or what your friends are doing, or what worked for Cousin Nancy. If you're working for them and their Whys, you will leave behind a vast sea of failed and unfinished projects.

WRITING EXERCISE: LET IT GO

Think of three things you've told yourself—or someone else—you'd do, but probably won't. They can be little things, like detailing your car, or big things, like volunteering to run a neighborhood watch group in your community. Maybe you won't get to cleaning the car before your spouse does it for you. Or maybe you said yes to the neighborhood watch group because you felt like you should, but now you're not giving it your best—or you're letting it cause stress in your home and steal time from other responsibilities.

Alright, so you have your list: three things you committed yourself to, one way or another. But you probably won't actually do them, or at least not the way they need to be done.

Accept it. Accept it with detachment and compassion. Then brainstorm some ethical ways to let go of each commitment.

Maybe you can pay the extra five dollars for detailing when you go to the car wash. Maybe you can offer to do a chore you don't mind, but your wife can't stand, in exchange for her cleaning the car (Just make sure it's something you'll actually do!). It's okay to tell someone you need to scale back your commitments. While no one will be glad to hear you're stepping down from the neighborhood watch, it's far better than continuing in a role where you feel you're constantly letting people down.

Every time you find yourself feeling stretched thin, break out your to-do list. Make a list of your roles in your office, family, and community. Identify a few you can let go, and find a responsible way to do so. You're not doing any favors by holding onto a commitment you won't fulfill.

A FEW LAST WORDS

If you take nothing else from this section, let it be this: to stay organized and on top of your responsibilities, you must be true to yourself.

You need to figure out who you are and how your brain works, and tailor your organizing system to your strengths. From the tools you use to the time of day you use them, who you are should inform every decision you make. ADHD already works against you so much of the time. Don't waste more time and energy working against yourself. If a tool or system doesn't feel right, you probably won't stick with it for the long haul.

Be warned, even the best system can't make you a superhero. To stay organized and sane, you'll need to become well-versed in saying no. If you're surrounded by unfinished projects, ask yourself why that might be. Are you stretched thin by a full plate of personal and professional commitments? Are you asking yourself to take on a challenging project, like a home renovation, that doesn't actually interest you? All these things put a drag on your productivity and mental energy. Instead of saying yes and doing things because you think you should, figure out how they serve your Why. If they don't, find a responsible way to bow out. No one, and especially no one with ADHD, has time or energy for everything.

KEY TAKEAWAYS

- Get to know yourself, and let who you are inform every decision you make. If it doesn't feel right, it probably isn't right for you.

- Try to ignore what works for everyone else and what you think others expect of you. Do what you need to do to lead a productive, happy, and responsible life.

- Be realistic about what you can accomplish and how. Others will respect you more if you are true to yourself and say no when appropriate, rather than if you try to do too much and fail to follow through.

RULE #2:
YOU NEED A CONTAINER
(AND IT CANNOT BE INSIDE YOUR
BRAIN)

CONTAINMENT BEFORE CONTROL

For those panicked souls who just arrived breathless and disheveled from the earlier chapter titled *Your Guide to This Book*, welcome. Have a seat. Take a few deep breaths and prepare for some heavy lifting. Don't forget about *Rule #1* and all the chapters before this one! They hold the keys to your long-term success.

If you've been with us the whole time, high fives all around. You now stand on solid ground to start the physical process of digging out of your mess.

As I said at the beginning of this book, you need to quell your feeling of panic if you want to stand a chance of putting your life in order. Surveying a disaster zone won't leave you with much zest for making progress. For me, it led to that Lost Room I told you about earlier.

That's where containment comes in. Before we can manage the chaos, we must begin to contain it. Otherwise it's too big and too intimidating. Start by getting all the loose stuff sorted into a system of containers. This will expose that floor that desperately needs cleaning while allowing you to work incrementally to create a system to manage it all. A big visual change will show you that you're making progress and reduce your feelings of futility.

Containment is not a solution. It's a start. Taking a laundry basket and filling it with all the unopened mail sitting around your house is a huge milestone. Give yourself permission to feel proud for doing it. Then figure out how to make sure future incoming mail lands in a consistent, well-defined place and gets opened and processed in a timely manner. But let's not think about that now. It gets its own section later in the book. It's called *Rule #3*. For now, focus on gathering and sorting what you have so you can clean and begin to deal with one thing at a time.

Back in the bad old days of chaos and disorder, I was drowning in piles. My problems all led back to piles: piles of stuff filling my house, a pile of sticky notes four layers thick on my desk, and thoughts piling on top of each other in my head. To make any progress, I had to defeat the piles. I had to contain everything: email, magazines, ideas, utility bills, toothbrushes, promises I'd made to others. For everything, I needed to find the appropriate container.

You need to as well if you want to dig your way out of the mess. Containers will help you both consolidate your tasks — all your unopened mail will now be in one place — and break them into manageable chunks. A huge mess is just that. A huge mess put into containers will give you something to hold onto, literally and figuratively.

KEY TAKEAWAYS

- A sprawling, uncontained mess looks too overwhelming and will keep you from making (or seeing) progress.

- Sorting your stuff into containers will allow you to clean the surfaces underneath.

- Once everything is sorted and contained, you can choose what to work on first/next.

RESPECT AND FEAR THE PILE

Where there's an uncontained pile, there's something waiting to be lost.

My first office had a big metal desk with an even bigger table alongside it. Today I'd look at that setup and immediately say, "That's too much horizontal surface." At the time it felt like a luxurious amount of space. And large horizontal surfaces *can* be luxurious. They're also a thing to be respected and feared, and that big table caused me more anxiety than it ever returned in utility.

Every time I needed to find something — a weekly report, a flyer, a payment request form, a book that belonged to someone else — I'd end up in a panic. The entire surface of the table was always burdened with several inches of paper. Finding one piece of paper usually meant going through each stack. As I grew more panicked in my search for the missing document, I'd come across other important papers I'd forgotten, and my panic would increase even more.

Ditto with the sticky notes on my desk. I kept so many, they'd often overlap. One can't-forget reminder would hide another. I lived every day on the verge of losing or forgetting something catastrophic.

If this level of stress was enough to discourage us from piling, we'd all keep tidy homes and offices. But we pile for a reason, which varies from pile to pile. Often, piles form because we lack a system for dealing with incoming items, or because the home or landing pad for those items is too inconvenient. Some people, and a disproportionate number of people with ADHD, have a significant aversion to putting anything out of sight, lest it slip permanently out of mind. These reasons for piling overpower our motivation to get organized.

The trick here is to store your stuff intentionally, categorically, and tidily. You may still have piles. Sometimes we need a stack of magazines in the living room or a collection of shoes near the door. But we can't allow those piles to take over. A pile has its own gravitational pull. It says, "It's okay to dump stuff here." Therefore, if you must have a pile, its purpose must be narrow and clear. You can't accept piles as a way of weaseling out of dealing with something (e.g. junk mail, a bag of hand-me-downs for the kids, etc.). If the piles aren't contained, they will never be managed.

In the following chapters, I'll talk about containing six major categories of stuff:

- Literal stuff, of the variety that's choking every horizontal surface in your home.
- Thoughts and ideas.
- Your schedule.
- Information.
- Incoming stuff that must be processed and dealt with.
- Distractions and hyperfocus black holes (we'll learn about these later).

All of it needs a container where it will not get lost and it will not contribute to the loss or misplacement of other stuff.

CONTAIN YOUR STUFF

The clothes were everywhere.

Despite my best efforts — which included, interchangeably: nagging, reminding, insisting, or just cleaning them up myself — my husband managed to keep several surfaces in our bedroom covered with clothes. The top of his dresser was the worst, always concealed under a heap of shirts, jeans, and hoodies.

I finally pressed him on the *why*, not the *what*. Why, I asked, couldn't he put the clothes in the hamper or closet where they belonged?

"I'm going to wear them again," he said. He didn't want to replace them in the closet because he'd already worn them and he didn't want me to skip them on laundry day. He didn't want to put them in the laundry because he might wear them again. Because they lacked a home, he tossed them in the first place he could find.

Since that day, I've made a point of getting to the bottom of why a system is failing, rather than nagging my family about the failure itself.

We had a similar struggle with stuff piled on the back of the toilet in our bathroom. My husband kept his toiletries there, but I wanted it all put away in the cabinet or under the sink. Every once in a while, I'd set off an avalanche and everything from the back of the toilet would clatter to the floor. I'd fly into a rage as I cleaned up the mess. But again, he wasn't trying to make a mess, and he didn't want the system — storing our personal items on a shelf in the cabinet — to fail. I just had to ask the right question: instead of "Can you *please*?" I had to ask an honest "Why aren't you?"

Many ADHD households struggle with clutter. Sometimes it's because we have too much stuff, but not always. Traditional organizing and tidying wisdom leads many ADHD families toward storage systems that make us uncomfortable.

My experiences cohabitating with my husband in the early years of our marriage gave me my first look into the world of visual thinkers and how they must organize their lives. Many people with ADHD are visually oriented, for whatever reason (I'm not, hence the learning curve). Poor memory and attention regulation also lead us to focus our tunnel vision on what we can perceive right now. This leaves out the past, the future, and everything else we can't see. When something is out of sight, it is truly out of mind.

Have you guessed yet why my husband never once put his shaving supplies away in the bathroom cabinet? He is what Judith Kolberg and Kathleen Nadeau refer to in their book *ADD-Friendly Ways to Organize Your Life* as an "out of sight out of mind person" (OOSOOM).[17] Objects out of sight may as well not exist.

If you live with a visually-oriented ADHDer, don't underestimate the perils of OOSOOM. Ignoring it and trying to push a system that relies on hidden storage may result in an environment where nothing gets put away.

PUT A BASKET ON IT

After investigating why things weren't getting put away in our home, I came to a breakthrough discovery: baskets. I put one on the back of the toilet, and my husband returned his toiletries to it every morning after getting ready for work. I put one in our bedroom for his clothes, and he never left a stray piece of clothing laying around again. I got fed up with magazines lurking all over our living and dining room, so I purchased a basket to store them on an end table. For every clutter hotspot, a basket has been 90 percent of the solution for us.

---

17   (Kolberg & Nadeau, 2002)

You can find attractive baskets just about anywhere: Target, craft stores, and IKEA, to name a few. Some are pricey, but the most affordable — usually plastic or metal, not wicker — can often be found in that little $1-$3 area just inside Target's front door.

If stuff keeps collecting in the same spot, there's a reason. That reason is unlikely to disappear unless you identify the cause and make the appropriate adjustments. While legitimizing it with a pretty container may feel like you're admitting defeat, you're not. This is effective problem-solving, and it's going to remove an unsightly clutter pile from your life.

POLICE YOUR BASKETS RUTHLESSLY

A word of caution about using baskets to organize your home and beat clutter: make sure each basket has *only one purpose*, and strictly regulate its contents. Baskets and open containers provide an excellent option for people who suffer from OOSOOM anxiety and refuse to use hidden storage. They also provide a lazy shortcut for people who don't feel like putting things away where they belong. Remain vigilant, lest your lovely baskets become black holes of clutter and despair.

Of course, somewhere along the way your lovely baskets will become just that. Prepare yourself now so you won't feel defeated and angry later. But also keep that vigilance alive. After you fix the mess, reinforce the rules.

Each basket or container should hold one type of item. You should know what to find in the basket, and which basket to look in when you need to find something. If you have a basket for magazines, make sure your kids don't start using it to stash their artwork. Never sweep a huge mess from a tabletop or floor into a big basket to deal with later. Open storage is a critical tool for organizing your life. It is not a shortcut.

WHEN A BASKET WON'T DO, TRY AN OPEN SHELF

It's likely your piles extend far beyond what can be contained in a basket. If you live in an ADHD household, or even just an exceptionally visually-oriented household, you may notice your family doesn't put anything away. Ever.

Remember *Rule #1* and accept the reality here. If you're up against ADHD, you may not be able to force the issue. You have to accept that in your home's current configuration, these items may never get put away, no matter how much anyone nags, bribes, or yells about it. Don't let that get you down. It's a fact, and facts lead us to solutions. Stop working on your coercion skills, especially because your loved ones may already *want* to put things away. Instead, work on a solution that honors the reality of your home.

This reality may include a lot of open storage, where you can see items even after they're neatly put away. Examples include:

- Using an open cube shelf, such as IKEA's popular KALLAX line, instead of drawers to store (folded!) clothes.
- Hanging clothing on a rolling garment rack.
- Ditching your filing cabinet in favor of an open file rack for your hanging files.
- Storing kitchen utensils in an attractive vase or bowl next to the stove.
- Using clear plastic drawers and containers to store supplies in a craft area.
- Installing a large pegboard in the garage or workshop instead of storing tools out of sight.

You may find that you (or a messy family member) don't actually enjoy having junk laying all over your desk, workbench, or kitchen counter. You don't love storing your clean laundry in the same basket you used to carry it from the dryer. What you love is being able to see those things. When you adopt storage that allows you to see them all the time, your brain will be more willing to let you put them away.

MAKE CLOSED STORAGE MORE ACCESSIBLE

Even when something lives in out-of-sight storage in our home, that storage is ADHD- and visual-thinker-friendly. I pay attention to how often an item gets used, who will be responsible for putting it away, and whether the contents of the closed storage are easy to discern from the outside.

Each item must have a clearly defined home. That home also needs to make sense and feel user-friendly. Generally speaking, an item's frequency of use should determine its ease of storage. Most people will exert the necessary effort to get out a tool if they really need it. But then the job is done and motivation to put it away drops to zero. Remember, motivation is a bigger hurdle for people with ADHD than it is for others. If you use something often, make sure it's easy enough to put away when you're done.

Minimalist though I may be, we have duplicates of a few key tools in our home. We have a pair of general-use scissors on each floor of the house. We used to have just one pair, but found ourselves searching for them on a regular basis. Everyone uses the scissors, usually for something quick, but no one tackles a flight of stairs to put them away when they're done. *Rule #1*: you must make peace with reality. That's just the way it is. There may be a few items you need to duplicate to make sure they get put away in a predictable place every time.

Just like I buy duplicates and offer open storage for items the whole family uses, I treat my things differently than others'. Unlike my husband, I'm not a highly visual person. I dislike clutter, and don't mind putting something out of sight as long as I have decent clues to help me find it later. Rather than keep everything in open storage, I prioritize keeping my husband's supplies in an easy-to-see location because he will benefit most from this. His toiletries stay out in a basket in the bathroom, while mine live in the medicine cabinet. Both of us put them away after each use.

We also make liberal use of labels. This reinforces a specific home for an item, but also lets others know where to find it. Have you ever turned the house upside down looking for an item you remember putting in a really good place? I've learned this "really good place" moment usually predicts a decreased likelihood of finding the item when I look for it later. Lightning never strikes the same place twice.

I'm a big fan of those heavy-duty plastic totes with the handles that lock over the top. Target, Walmart, and big-box hardware stores have them in a variety of colors. We use them to organize holiday decorations, clothes, camping supplies, and the like in our basement storage room. I love how they stand up to pretty much anything and can be stacked as high as I can comfortably reach. Each one of these totes has a label on it with the contents — no exceptions. Otherwise, the room would be a mess from people rummaging to find stuff, dumping items on the floor because they didn't feel like finding the right bin to put them away, or just shoving unrelated items into the first bin they found.

Whenever something goes into a container, I label it, even if I'm convinced I couldn't possibly forget the purpose or contents. We invested in a P-Touch labeler to streamline the labeling process, and I've never looked back. When in doubt, use a label.

BOTTOM LINE: WORK WITH REALITY AND MAKE IT EASY

Remember, clutter hotspots shouldn't trigger your nagging or lecturing reflex. Treat these failures of your organizational system (or lack thereof) as clues. They will lead you to the best solution if you ask the right questions.

To do this, you need to get to know your brain and your family's brains. Provide containers and storage options that work with your brain, not against it. Don't ask more of yourself or your family than you will actually give.

In other words, make it easy to find the things you need in your home, and to put them away where they belong when you're done. Use baskets, open storage, and labels to contain and categorize your stuff. If you're overwhelmed by the magnitude of the task, start with containment as a first step. Sort the mess into containers, even if those containers are temporary. Don't ask your brain to look at an entire room full of clutter and form a solution. Break it down, sort it, and contain it. Know your brain, accept your reality, and create a solution that offers the path of least resistance.

KEY TAKEAWAYS

- Never keep your stuff in a big pile with no container around it — use baskets, bins, etc. to set boundaries for those piles.

- If you use baskets or open bins for storage, make sure those containers are used for one purpose *only*.

- If you or your family aren't putting things away where they belong, quit nagging and ask why instead.

- Don't try to force visual thinkers to store their things out of sight, out of mind — they won't do it.

- When you need to put something in closed/hidden storage, use labels to enforce proper use of that container and let others know what to find in there.

- Always accept reality and create solutions based on your household's unique needs.

CONTAIN YOUR INCOMING TASKS

If you're an adult with a job and a home, you probably have a constant, overwhelming flow of to-dos. I know I do, and I don't even commute to an office to do my work.

Many of our to-do items come from physical stuff, which needs a physical container: receipts, mail, a broken toy, and a note from your child's teacher all fit this bill.

And then there's email.

EMAIL: THE CONTAINER THAT GROWS, AND GROWS, AND GROWS...

If we let our snail mail pile up for months (or years) on end, what happens? We start running out of space to put new mail. It's a problem you can see. Mail requires a physical place to land, and it stares us in the face every time we walk by.

Email is a whole different beast. I've met people with inboxes topping 100,000 *unread* messages. Talk about anxiety-inducing! By the end of this book, I hope to have convinced you of the importance of *emptying your inbox to zero* (yes, you read that correctly) at least once every few days.

However.

An email inbox with literally thousands of unread messages is exactly the kind of thing that makes people — and especially people with ADHD — view Inbox Zero as nothing but a fantasy. How are you supposed to force yourself to deal with all that? Your ADHD, and your seeming inability to deal with email at anywhere close to the rate you receive it, is what got you here in the first place. Emptying your inbox every few days would mean keeping up with new messages *plus* doing a lot of catch-up work. That's a tall order for anyone, let alone a person with ADHD.

Declaring Bankruptcy on Your Email

What you need, more than to reach that unattainable goal of catching up, is to give yourself a fresh start. Let's be realistic: the email at the very bottom of that mountain is probably obsolete by now. Even if it was important at some point, it's meaningless today. Except it's not completely meaningless. It's standing between you and a clean inbox. You're depriving yourself of a fresh start because you'll never catch up, and you'll never catch up because you're depriving yourself of a fresh start.

"How much stuff in your life has gotten unmanageable simply because you decided at some point that you were too behind to ever make a difference?" asks writer and podcaster Merlin Mann in his popular blog, *43 Folders*. Mann recommends a radical approach: relegate your entire inbox to a so-called "DMZ" and give yourself that fresh start — starting immediately. Mann's process is simple:[18]

1. Open your email program and create a new folder called "DMZ"

2. Go to your email inbox and Select All (You might alternatively choose all email older than *n* days)

3. Drag those emails from your inbox into the DMZ folder

4. Go, and sin no more.

Simple, yet terrifying. While this shouldn't give you license to pretend the DMZ doesn't exist, you may be surprised by what you're able to let go. I once introduced a boss to the

---

18 (Mann, 2006)

DMZ, and she gleefully deleted all emails older than six months. The rest of the office was aghast. And yet, the world didn't end. We're talking about emails over six months old. Even if you're not the CEO of a company, you have to trust that if it was critically important, someone would've addressed it with you through other channels already.

If you're sitting on an inbox of hundreds, even thousands, of unsorted/unprocessed emails, I'm giving you permission to remove them. Don't delete them (yet) if you don't feel you can. But put them somewhere other than your inbox—like a DMZ folder. Your email inbox, like your real-world inboxes, is a place for incoming tasks and information. You wouldn't leave 50,000 unopened pieces of mail in your living room. Don't do it in your electronic space, either. Email is a primary means of communication for many people and organizations. You can't afford to bury yourself so deeply.

Of course, once your old emails have been banished to the DMZ, you'll have to keep new messages from piling up again. We'll get to that in *Rule #3: You Need a System That Works.*

A PLACE FOR INCOMING 'STUFF' TO LAND

Once upon a time, I lived in a sea of sticky notes. Every time I thought of something I needed to do or remember, I wrote it on a sticky note and stuck it to my desk or computer monitor. This was an improvement upon my past life, where I had not learned the necessity of writing so many things down. But the sticky notes also added visual clutter, and I often forgot to look at them.

I was barely out of my teens when I learned I needed to write everything down if I wanted to remember it. At my first job out of college, I purchased a day planner like the ones I'd found at the university bookstore. I used this to record deadlines and important events. I came up with a system for taking notes at meetings, indicating with a star, instead of a bullet point, items that required future action on my part. I also used this system in the notebooks I carried everywhere with me.

The distributed nature of this system was its downfall. I recorded most of the items requiring action, but the records were all over the place: on a sticky note beneath three other sticky notes on my desk. In a notebook I'd just filled, and I forgot to transfer the information to my planner or new notebook. In a day planner. In a stack of papers I left on my computer's keyboard so it would get in my way tomorrow morning (and thus remind me to handle them immediately). In a stack of mail on the dining room table.

It was too easy to lose, forget, or overlook something important.

Once our space becomes cluttered, we encounter more barriers to dealing with the problem. Cleaning up a cluttered space can feel very overwhelming for a person with ADHD. As we become more overwhelmed, we find ways to avoid it, maybe by leaving the room, turning on the TV, or staring at our smart phone. Our avoidance begets more clutter, which begets more overwhelm, which begets even more avoidance, and so on.[19]

People with ADHD need to write a lot of things down, and we need a lot of reminders. That's okay. The problem begins when we scatter these notes and reminders all over our home and office. We keep a broken toy on the kitchen counter so we won't forget to fix it. We stack school papers on the dining room table so we'll remember to sign them and return them to our children's school. We cover our desk so thickly with sticky notes, they fail to mean anything to us.

The key is to create a few central containers for these incoming tasks, which you will process regularly. Don't make a mess. That will overwhelm your brain, and you'll lose something important. Try to funnel your incoming channels, or sources of information and tasks that require action from you, into as few buckets as possible. Let's call a bucket (or container) of actionable stuff an inbox.

Here are my primary incoming channels:

- Papers from my child's school and my work.
- Snail mail.
- Email.
- Voicemail.
- Text messages.
- Private messages via Facebook & other social media.
- Handwritten notes/ideas.
- Physical objects that need repair or a new home.

If I allowed each of these to serve as its own inbox, that would be too overwhelming. Text messages, voicemail, and social media present a special challenge because they lack a feature to "mark unread" or keep their notifications in front of my eyes after I read them for the first time. I forget about these communications as soon as something else distracts me. To keep everything under control, I use my sticky notes (I always have some within a few steps, if not arm's reach) to transfer them to my regular inbox. Converting text messages and other electronic inputs to sticky notes allows me to send everything to one of these three inboxes:

---

19   (Kolberg & Nadeau, 2002)

Email Inbox

Most people have at least one email inbox with a significant number of action items coming in daily.

Despite having several email addresses, I feed all email into one central account. When I didn't work for myself, I still maintained only two email inboxes: my work email and my personal email.

Many people choose to keep several email addresses: one for junk mail and promotions, one for friends and family, one for sending out resumes, etc. If this system feels indispensable to you, I won't tell you to delete the extra accounts, but I strongly urge you to forward all mail to one account. In other words, find a way to *check* only one account — two if you have a separate work email address — even if the outside world sees more than that. Gmail makes this easy to do in its settings.

A word about corporate email (i.e. an email address assigned by your employer): many people I've met tend to ask others to email them at one address or another based on which they maintain more responsibly. For example, "Send it to my work email, I'm so behind on my other one," or "I'll email you from my personal account because I can check it more easily at home." This is almost always a bad idea for your own task flow, not to mention inconsiderate to those you're asking to accommodate you. If you receive email at an address and there's an expectation you will read and respond to it, you should maintain it responsibly. You should have a manageable number of email inboxes and you should be using them for their established purpose. No more, no less.

Not convinced on the grounds of task flow and clarity alone? Remember most people will change jobs at some point in their lives. In some industries, downsizing and layoffs can occur with little warning. Imagine you've given everyone the impression they should email you at work if it's important, only to find you'll be moving on before you'd originally predicted.

More importantly, take it from a former IT manager: a corporate email account generally carries with it no expectation of privacy. This is not to say your boss or the IT department is reading all your emails. No one has the time or interest in that under normal circumstances. But you very likely signed something with your new hire paperwork acknowledging that all communications from your work email address may be subject to monitoring. Even with a small, tight-knit company, I've been in the position of having to monitor someone's email communications or cut off their account access without notice. It's not unheard of, and — again, practical considerations aside — I always advise against using your work email for personal communications.

Office Inbox

I keep a small inbox basket in my office, and it serves several purposes. For one, I need a place to put all the sticky notes I use to scribble random ideas while I sit at my desk. Many of my best, or at least my most persistent, ideas come to me while I'm supposed to be working on something else. To clear them from my mind and focus on the task at hand, I write them down and drop them into my inbox. I also open all our family's mail in my office. It's where a lot of work happens, and so I generate a lot of to-dos that need a place to go.

I recommend having a physical inbox where you do most of your work. If your office is outside the home, you'll need a physical inbox there as well. Some items may need to move between home and work. Several office supply manufacturers sell durable plastic file folders that work quite well for transporting papers and notes.

Front Door Inbox

In keeping with my "containers as near as we need them" rule, I have an inbox basket right inside our front door. I drop the mail in here every day, but it's also centrally located for my family. Every few days, I empty this inbox into my office inbox for processing.

Consider that you may not be the only one to put things in your physical inbox. At five years old, my son already knows if he wants me to do or remember something, he must put it in my inbox. When my husband saves receipts from credit card transactions, he drops them in there. We all occasionally jot a reminder on a sticky note and put it in the front door inbox.

The critical point here is, I have a collection basket in our living room, right by the front door, to collect incoming stuff requiring action. It's convenient for my family, who use it to give me action items in a non-cluttered, non-overwhelming way.

If your job or home life is such that you have a lot of stuff coming in from other people, you may want to consider a separate inbox just for that purpose. However, I caution against getting too specific with inbox types. I find that if I know what's in there — e.g. "Oh, those are all credit card receipts" — it's easier to justify procrastination. If I keep one inbox for everything coming in, I see a half-full basket and think, "It's time for me to process all of that before it gets out of control." I've tried a separate collection point for credit card receipts in the past. I don't think I ever had fewer than six months' worth of receipts in there. In the next section, you'll be setting up a system for dealing with your incoming tasks. Better to create a system you can trust, and not undermine it by pre-sorting your inbox.

BOTTOM LINE: FUNNEL YOUR 'IN' CHANNELS INTO AS FEW CONTAINERS AS POSSIBLE, AND MAKE THEM APPROACHABLE

Don't keep your incoming to-dos scattered all over your home and office. Contain these items in as few receptacles as you can get away with so you're less likely to lose track of something important. Remember that people with ADHD have trouble holding multiple things in their mind at once. Even though our surroundings often appear scattered, we don't function well this way. If you put your most important reminders on sticky notes stuck to your computer monitor, you'll forget your other inbox exists. Containment is key.

As you work on containment, don't ask anything unrealistic of yourself or others. If others frequently give you things to do, provide an easy-to-use central collection point like my front door inbasket. If you've let your email inbox get out of control, don't give up on emptying it — empty it today. Ask a friend or family member to sit with you and help you get a clean start. Let go of anything that has become obsolete. Be realistic about non-critical stuff you're never going to do. Simplify until the problem begins to feel manageable.

KEY TAKEAWAYS

- Don't let an inbox overflowing with the previous year's mess keep you from dealing with what comes in today.

- If your inbox has gotten out of control, empty it: get rid of anything obsolete or unrealistic.

- Don't use anything out of sight, out of mind as an inbox. This includes your smart phone's disappearing text message, voicemail, and social media notifications. Record the important ones on sticky notes and put them in your physical inbox for later.

- Collect incoming things to do at as few points as possible so no inbox gets overlooked.

- Use as many inboxes as you need to collect to-do items effectively.

- Consider other people who give you things to do and make it easy for them to put these items in your inbox.

CONTAIN YOUR THOUGHTS

There are few feelings worse than forgetting something important, especially when we hurt or disappoint our family, friends, or colleagues as a result. These people's opinions matter to us. We depend on our relationships with them. We don't want to let them down, and yet we so often do.

Even when we're not letting other people down, we frustrate ourselves. We think of the same ideas repeatedly, never remembering at a time when we can act.

Imagine a sieve full of a weird combination of stuff, some of it valuable, some not: uncooked lentils, diamonds, plastic beads, and some heirloom jewelry passed down from your great-great-grandmother. Now imagine watching all of it fall through the sieve's holes. Does the sieve care whether you lose something worthless, expensive, or irreplaceable? Nope.

My memory is like that sieve. Many people with ADHD have a memory like that sieve. We also have a beating heart and a conscience. Sometimes that sucks.

People without ADHD don't understand this. How could we forget something so important? We remembered the drop date for *Stranger Things 2* on Netflix, didn't we?

I know. It doesn't make sense. We wish the important stuff wouldn't fall through the sieve. We wish the people we love wouldn't take our catastrophic screw-ups personally. We wish everyone knew just how much we really care, and how much pain and self-loathing we've experienced in our lives because our brains betray us nearly every day.

This pain can lead people with ADHD to do terrible things. It can keep us from pursuing close relationships, or it can break those relationships down.

Even if we lived in total isolation, forgetting would still hurt. It's hard to be successful when you're using your mental energy to generate the same idea over and over again. It's hard to use any of your ideas when you can't remember them at the appropriate time.

If we want to live a life that's tolerable to us and to others, we need to seal up that sieve-like memory.

I've learned it the hard way again and again: I need to write everything down. *Everything.* If I catch myself thinking, "That's too important, I know I won't forget it," that's a huge red flag. It means I absolutely will forget it, and I'll be twice as frustrated when I do.

Not only do I have to write everything down, I have to do this immediately — like in a matter of seconds. As a result, the distance between me and an idea container must be short. Ideally in arm's reach, but certainly never outside the room.

As you can imagine, I've had to let go of my desire to appear sane. I maintain writable surfaces all over my house: sticky notes, dry erase boards, chalkboards, you name it. Even the bathroom mirror. I carry sticky notes in my bag and there's a notepad in the center console of my car. I call this "storing my brain outside my head." People give me weird looks about the sticky notes, and I've been asked why I have dry erase markers in my bathroom. I know it's not normal. I've never found a dry erase marker in someone else's bathroom, but I don't mind looking like a weirdo.

I do all this because I hate feeling like a jerk. I grew up being called selfish and inconsiderate, even though I consider myself a loving, helpful, and empathetic person. Remember the writing exercise about finding your Why and facing the dissonance between the person you are and the person others see? If there's anyone out there who considers me a good friend, spouse, parent, or anything else, it's because I never trust myself. I always, always, always assume I'll forget.

POTTY TRAIN YOUR BRAIN

If I could name the single most important thing I've learned as a person with ADHD, it's this: I can never trust my brain.

Allow me to digress into parent-talk for a moment here. There's a potty-training method for toddlers that people call the three-day method. Parents take three days off from the outside world, roll up the area rugs, and strip their toddler down to his birthday suit. Every time he begins to empty his bladder onto the floor, you whisk him to the potty, ideally before he finishes his business. You celebrate every tiny drop that makes it into that potty. By the end of the third day, you may return to your life with a potty-trained child in tow.

This sounded great to me. Several parent friends had highly recommended it. However, if you have ADHD and might potty train a child at some point in the future, let me give you a piece of advice: avoid the three-day method.

To be clear, my kid may have been able to ace it. I'll never know. This process required such constant vigilance, it quickly stressed my attention span to the breaking point. I had a complete meltdown by lunchtime on the second day. My brain wasn't made for the three-day method. While my son seemed relatively unfazed, I felt like I'd spent 24 hours in a CIA torture chamber.

My brain, it turns out, is more like the naked toddler getting ready to pee on the floor. It requires constant vigilance. I need to be on the lookout for ideas all the time, or I'll lose them. At the first sign of an idea, I have to whisk it to an appropriate container.

That's what I mean when I say I can't trust my brain. It's great at generating ideas and solving problems. That, as far as I'm concerned, is what brains are for. Storing information and recalling it at the most useful moment? Not so much.

As I said before, I have idea containers all over my house. No more than three to five steps away at any time, I want a surface I can write on.

If you want to get serious about organizing your thoughts, ideas, projects, and important information, organize your home such that a thought container is never farther away than your attention span is long.

THE DIFFERENCE BETWEEN THOUGHT CONTAINERS AND INBOXES

As David Allen writes in *Getting Things Done*, "you should have as many [inboxes] as you need and as few as you can get by with." Allen describes various containers and collection points — cell phone voicemail, email, physical in-baskets, loose-leaf notebooks, etc. — as relatively equal in the GTD system. People with ADHD, especially those with severe memory issues, should consider breaking this down into two levels. We need far more containers than we can have inboxes.

You'll remember I don't consider my voicemail an inbox, per se. It's a collection point from which I take notes and drop those handwritten sheets into a physical inbox. I maintain only three main collection points for incoming information that needs to be processed: email inbox, office inbox, front-door inbox. However, I always have a thought container within reach. This is a two-part strategy: err on the side of excess when it comes to collection tools (i.e. thought containers) such as sticky notes, notebooks, chalkboards, etc. Then, err on the side of caution with actual inboxes, which you must monitor and empty with some frequency. Never limit yourself when collecting thoughts and information, but funnel these down to as few inboxes as possible.

TOOLS OF THE TRADE: THE MANY FORMS OF THE THOUGHT POTTY

What follows is a lengthy-yet-far-from-exhaustive list of containers you can use to capture your thoughts before they drift away.

Sticky Notes

Sticky notes are by far my most heavily-used thought container. I purchase them in bulk packages intended for large offices and keep some in every room of my house. You'll find them hidden, along with a ballpoint pen, in the kitchen, in my car's glove compartment, on my bedside table, and in my bag. I'm never without quick and easy access to a sticky note. They needn't be fancy. I swear by the three-inch-square, unlined, original Post-It. I don't color code them, but I do purchase the recycled version and recycle my notes when I finish with them because I use so many.

Don't be shy about your sticky notes. As opposed to a notebook, they easily detach from their pad and can exist on their own or in groups. You can drop them directly into your inbox, use them as a temporary label for another container, leave a note for someone else, stick them to another document, or stick them to a surface as a reminder. After sticking one on my car radio to remind me to disarm our home alarm before going inside, I noted a decrease in embarrassing videos emailed to my husband by the alarm system.

'Trouble Tickets' and Other Specialized Forms

At a job providing IT support to a small office, my colleagues gave me flak for my attachment to red tape. They wondered why they should fill out a form when they could just stop by for a chat. Well, I wasn't doing busy work just for fun. I have ADHD, after all. I was trying to make sure I helped people when they needed me.

People often stopped me by the coffeemaker to share their latest computer woes. This system worked great when I could solve a problem by giving advice while refilling my mug. It fell apart for anything that required follow-up. Our breakroom was well-stocked with coffee, creamer, and a variety of hand-me-down ceramic mugs, but it lacked thought containers. By the time I took the 20 steps back to my office, I'd forgotten all about the computer conversation. Of course, the person asking for help would not forget. I dreaded those coffee station walk-bys because I grew to associate them with complaints to my boss about my lack of responsiveness.

To solve this problem, I created an IT help request form. The form collected the person's name, a description of the problem, and some indication of the level of urgency *for them*. People chafed against this all the time, but I insisted: this isn't bureaucracy for its own sake. I literally will not remember to help you otherwise. I would even fill it out on your behalf, if I was headed back to my office and felt near enough to my stack of request forms. It was a specialty thought container, a guided recording process that ensured a specific, complete set of information made it into my inbox.

If your job requires you to accept many of the same type of request — e.g. account creation, tech support, website update, phone call, etc. — and you don't already have a template to guide these requests, consider creating one with your favorite word processing program. It might feel stuffy and bureaucratic at first, but standardizing a request process on paper takes the pressure off and ensures you have all the information you need.

At home, trouble tickets and help requests work just as well, and they can be as formal or informal as you like. My husband has set up a trouble ticket system for our house. He writes software for a living, so this is the system he knows. We enter all maintenance issues, home improvement ideas, renovation projects, and the like into this database. We can also indicate whether one project depends upon, or blocks, another. For example, we couldn't install our new kitchen shelving until the kitchen renovation had come to a close. We use a piece of software called JIRA for this, but there are many project and ticket management solutions on the market to suit people at all levels of tech-savviness.

Feel free to have fun with request forms, especially at home. Allow your family to formally request special outings, restaurant or takeout meals, or changes to routines that aren't quite working. Explain that saving it in a predictable format will help you make these things happen for them. They may even thank you. A template can be very helpful for people who struggle to articulate thoughts in writing.

Thought Containers as Built-In Décor

For something you really can't misplace, try increasing your home's writable surfaces. I've used the small dry-erase boards popular in college dormitories to create portable, easily-repurposed note-taking surfaces.

Remember the dry erase markers in our bathroom? Two markers with magnetic lids have a permanent home clinging to the side of our medicine cabinet. They've raised some eyebrows, but before you laugh, remember there's a reason you have so many ideas in the shower.[20] You're relaxed, relatively free of distractions, and experiencing a nice dopamine rush from the hot water. Your brain is primed for idea generation.

The problem is, my ADHD and poor memory usually conspire to make me forget these ideas before I've even dried off. At first I tried keeping a waterproof notepad and pen in the shower, but this must've given my brain performance anxiety. I never used the waterproof paper. My solution: just write on the mirror. As soon as I hop out of the shower, I can scribble a note there to remind me what I was thinking.

The mirror is a great place for all kinds of things, like leaving a loving note or drawing for your spouse. When I worked in IT, my mirror notes reminded me to do early-morning server maintenance from home, before people started showing up at the office. Visitors occasionally spot our markers and join the fun, too.

Pinterest is full of trendy, beautiful "command centers" that will make your organizational system feel frumpy and inadequate. But don't feel like you need to create an interior design project for yourself. The key is to get off the ground with as little effort as possible. That's why, for us, taking a dry erase marker into the bathroom fits the bill perfectly.

If you want to get a little more ambitious, try chalkboard or dry erase paint for a wall or door in your home. Personally, I've had greater success with the chalkboard paint, but dry

---

20 (Widrich, 2017)

erase could be a better choice for those concerned about dust. Our house has old-fashioned wood doors with two big inset panels, and we've transformed the panels on one of them into chalkboard space for writing. This door lives in our kitchen, and it's my primary spot for jotting additions to my grocery list. We get tons of compliments on it. You could also mount an old picture frame to the wall as a border for a chalkboard or dry erase area. Just make sure you read the full instructions on the paint can so your project is both attractive and usable.

Checklists

In this case, I refer to a checklist not as a container for the tasks themselves, but for progress. You probably have several processes in your life that you repeat many times. For example:

- Packing and closing up your home before a vacation.
- Locking up the office if you're the last one to leave.
- Paying bills and balancing your checkbook.
- Replacing a credit card following a fraud incident.

Rather than try to keep all the steps in your brain — remember, this puts a strain on working memory, an area of weakness for people with ADHD — create a checklist. Refer to it at each step and mark tasks off as you go.

Your checklists will help you in several ways. First, you won't forget where you are in the process, which can lead to duplicating work or forgetting an important step. Second, a checklist makes it easier to ask for help. When I'm trying to remember the steps to a process, like packing for a vacation, I have an extremely low tolerance for interruptions. I don't want to break my chain of thought, lest I forget what I'm doing entirely. This makes interrupting with "how can I help" particularly problematic. Not only do I have to stop what I'm doing, I have to think through how I could include another person. Interruptions are reduced dramatically when helpers can refer to a central checklist. Whether you're working alone or with a team, a checklist is almost never a bad idea.

Like with the other thought containers, don't be shy with your checklists. Some of the smartest, most capable people in the world rely on them every day. Hospitals have seen dramatic drops in death and infection rates after implementing checklists that simply reiterate what doctors and nurses already know.[21]

---

21 (Vedantam, 2017)

Notebooks

I keep a small notebook in my clutch wallet and carry a larger one almost everywhere I go. These are for writing more complex ideas, taking notes at meetings, and doing work on the go (e.g. outlining blog posts or writing out a checklist).

While I couldn't live without my notebooks, I recommend using them judiciously. Don't use them for small to-dos or reminders that could fit on a sticky note. The notebook can feel like its own inbox: something you must make time to sit and process. And it's only as useful as its index. Before I found an airtight system for indexing handwritten notebooks and journals, I frequently lost action items in the pages. Sticky notes exist as individual items to be dealt with discretely. If your thought can fit on a sticky note, that is the most appropriate place to put it. If you're writing a page or two articulating your feelings on the most recent presidential election, you ought to open up a notebook.

Someday, Maybe

The Someday Maybe list comes from the GTD system. It provides a container for all the ideas you can't (or shouldn't) act upon right now. While you may be tempted to overlook it, don't. It's a lifesaver for people with ADHD. It preserves those exciting plans and ideas while giving you permission not to do them all at once.

Use your Someday Maybe list for everything you want but can't do or buy right now.[22] For example: big-ticket purchases, vacations, skill development, new hobbies, maybe even the things you promised in the introductory writing exercises that you'd let go.

This is especially important for people with ADHD, who may struggle to prioritize their project list for any number of reasons. We have a terrible time saying no to anything that sounds appealing, for one. The idea of delaying gratification or waiting until we have sufficient time, energy, or money simply does not occur to us in the heat of the moment. But even if we recognize something as not a priority right now, we may hesitate to put it off for fear of forgetting.

When I first started with GTD, I feared the Someday Maybe list would feel restrictive, like I had to force myself to put things there instead of on my active to-do lists. I wanted to build a storage ottoman now, today! I wanted to start planning a family camping trip immediately! And so on. Accepting Someday Maybe meant admitting I might have to wait.

---

22 (Allen, 2015)

In the end, Someday Maybe felt more liberating than anything else. When I gave myself permission to put a project, idea, or purchase on the Someday Maybe list, I felt unburdened. I didn't have to figure out how to fit it onto my already-full plate. It helped me with *Rule #1* (making peace with reality). And yet I didn't have to say goodbye forever. Someday Maybe is simply goodbye for now — and a place to remember when the time is right.

My Someday Maybe list lives in a very simple format, as a bulleted list in a Microsoft Word document. In a way, it may not quite fit in this section because I often populate it from sticky notes and other items in my inboxes. However, I couldn't write a chapter on containers without including it. It's like a treasure chest where you can keep those shiny, exciting ideas safe until you can act on them. If you have ADHD, or live with someone who does, you know how valuable this is.

Isn't There an App for All This?

A gadget-loving reader might notice I didn't include many electronic note-taking tools in this chapter. There are some great ones available — Evernote, Toodledo, Google Keep, and your smart phone's built-in notes app, to name a few — but I find computers and smart phones too distracting to serve as effective idea containers. When I unlock my phone screen, I rarely make it to my note-taking app. Several minutes later, I realize I'm checking my Instagram feed and have no idea why I grabbed my phone in the first place. A simple pen and paper works best for me.

Remember that ADHD gives you a weak filter for extraneous distractions. Our smartphones are designed to distract us. There may be people out there who have no trouble seeing a notification pop up on their phone and saying "maybe later" before proceeding with whatever they were doing. I doubt anyone who can do this has ADHD.

As I'll talk about later, I own a smartphone. They can be invaluable for people with ADHD. However, their utility can easily be overshadowed by their abundance of temptations and distractions. You alone will know, in time, how much smartphone use and reliance is healthy for you.

A FINAL NOTE: DON'T MISS THE INBOX

With all these notes flying around, it'd be easy to get overwhelmed. Here's where you bring everything you've learned in this chapter to bear.

It's not enough to extract your ideas from your brain and contain them on sticky notes. You must also contain the notes themselves. Without a central bucket or two to collect everything, sticky notes, notebooks, and even checklists simply become clutter. Once you capture your thoughts, be vigilant with them. Make sure they make it home.

KEY TAKEAWAYS

- Never let yourself get too far from a thought container.

- Don't be shy about your need to write everything down. Remembering important things will give you confidence in yourself, and others confidence in you. It's worth looking a little eccentric.

- If you can't act on an idea right now, keep it safe in your Someday Maybe list. This gives you freedom not to act.

- Be careful with electronic note-taking tools. Sometimes computers and smart phones add too many distractions.

- Make sure your many notes funnel into relatively few actual *inboxes*: containers you empty and act upon regularly.

CONTAIN YOUR SCHEDULE & OBLIGATIONS

"I would die if my calendar looked like that."

A friend had just peeked over my shoulder at my phone screen as we discussed a date for a future meeting. My calendar looked like it usually did: a sea of color-coded notes. Many days had so many items, they exceeded the capacity of the whole-month view on my phone's little screen.

This may look a bit overwhelming to the uninitiated, but I only include what I need to on my calendar. That is, information, appointments, and tasks that are only relevant to a specific day or range of days. I'm judicious with what I put on my calendar, but I don't leave anything off, either.

WHAT DOES IT MEAN TO BE A GOOD FRIEND?

Sometimes shame causes us to resist the tools that would help us feel organized and successful. Every time I add a note to my calendar, I'm admitting to myself I probably wouldn't remember it otherwise. This should reduce my anxiety. I can breathe easy knowing I won't forget my sister's birthday, right? But part of me also wants to remember my sister's birthday — *for real*. With my brain. And leaning hard on my calendar can make me feel like a fraud.

Let's talk for a moment about *kinkeeping*. Kinkeeping refers to the work that must be done to keep extended families connected. This work often falls on one person, and that person is usually female.[23] ADHD occurs in women about as often as it does in men, yet social expectations can be very different.

Let's face it: this is work. I'm our family's kinkeeper. I send our Christmas cards, wish people a happy birthday via text message or Facebook, do 90 percent of our gift shopping, plan family visits, and mediate conflicts. I keep track of what's happening in the lives of siblings, cousins, and other extended family, and make sure we acknowledge major events. I do this for both sides of the family. If anyone should receive communication directly from my husband, I remind him and ensure he does it. Kinkeepers provide social glue. Our work is something many people assume comes naturally, but it requires exceptional organization.

When kinkeepers fail, the emotional stakes are high. Broad kinkeeping responsibilities (that is, keeping track of a large social network) can conflict with other roles, such as household and career obligations. Unsurprisingly, these stresses are associated with increased depression.[24] As more women have taken on full-time work outside the home, the expectations of kinkeeping — still very gendered — leave us feeling drained.

I've folded kinkeeping into my obsessive organizational systems. When a close friend suffered a miscarriage, I stuck a sticky note to my phone before bed to remind me to text her and check in when I woke up. Most days, this makes me look like a good friend.

But sometimes I don't *feel* like a good friend. I wish I could remember this stuff on my own. No matter how much I love you, without my calendar and to-do list, you'd get the impression I never thought of you at all.

Maybe no one cares how I get there because the end result — someone feeling loved and remembered — matters most. On a good day, I believe that. When I let shame creep in, I see in myself a person who can't show even the most basic consideration for those I love without an extensive system of calendar reminders, apps, and handwritten notes.

And yet without me playing the role of kinkeeper, where would my family be? I need to stay more organized just to clear the bar as a responsible, self-respecting adult. I've made myself a perfect fit for this kinkeeping role. Everything gets dumped into my organization-

---

23 (Rosenthal, 1985)
24 (Gerstel & Gallagher, 1993)

al system, from the electric bill to my sister's 18th birthday. While that may sound cold in its egalitarianism, I never forget the electric bill or my sister's birthday. Ironically, because I *can* forget so much, I end up forgetting relatively little. I maintain a more airtight system than most people I know.

If you play any kinkeeping roles in your family, know the effort you make is never hollow. When you create an organized life for yourself, honor it for what it is: the glue that holds your family's social bonds together. So what if it's not all in your head? Your family will be better for it.

SO, WHAT GOES ON THE CALENDAR?

I kid you not, if something has a date attached, it's on my calendar. This includes, but is not limited to:

- **Deadlines**
  We're talking hard deadlines like filing taxes, getting an early bird rate on a conference registration, and registering my kid for dance class. But don't forget the squishy ones that usually get away, like when I tell someone, "I'll think about it and let you know next week." I write those on the calendar, too.

- **Anniversaries**
  Of course I have my own wedding and dating anniversaries on my calendar, but I include important friend and family stuff, too. When a friend lost her brother, there it went onto my Google Calendar so I could text her on the one-year anniversary to let her know I was thinking about her.

- **Birthdays**
  If someone has a birthday and I want to acknowledge it, it's on my calendar.

- **Appointments**
  Haircuts, play dates, recurring meetings, birthday parties, and absolutely any circumstance where I'll be expected to be at a specific location at a specific time. This also includes all my son's activities because I need to drive him. No exceptions, ever. If it's supposed to be a surprise or a secret, I create a fake name for the event on my calendar or use a Google calendar only I can view (you may not be surprised to learn I don't like surprises or secrets because they add extra layers of work and stress to my life).

- **Reminders**
  This one is related to deadlines, but it's even squishier than "I'll get back to you next week." I went hiking with my son on Mother's Day, and my mom expressed interested in joining us next year. I scrolled all the way to next April and wrote a note on my calendar: "Remind Mom about Mother's Day hike and see if she'd like to come visit that

weekend." This little stuff goes a long, long way. Once you shake the stigma of using your calendar like this, you can start feeling like the rock star you are.

Just like any other type of information I mention in this chapter, you cannot store this in your head. Time-sensitive information is perhaps the most important to get out of your head and into a well-maintained system.

It's also easy to start right now. Today. Don't go another minute without a calendar in your life. I highly recommend Google Calendar. It integrates with Gmail, so key events like airline reservations appear automatically. Because it's Google, you can search your entire calendar — past, present, and future — in a split second. It also stays safely backed up in the cloud, away from the physical hazards of everyday life.

While I do handwrite part of my calendar (I'll get to that in the next section) I store 100 percent of my time-sensitive information electronically. Even if you don't use Google Calendar, I encourage you to adopt something other than a paper planner, and not just because it's impossible to leave it on the bus by accident.

Electronic calendars have the tools to make your life easier. Managing a calendar can feel tedious. Anything that reduces that tedium and eliminates points of failure is your friend. Electronic calendars allow you to set and forget recurring events and filter out irrelevant information when you need to. Many things in my life, from birthdays to my favorite yoga class, repeat on a predictable schedule. Once I add them to the calendar and define that schedule, I'm done. My calendar will remind me of each occurrence.

Because that leads to a lot of stuff on the calendar, I also appreciate the ability to turn off a whole category of items. For example, I have a separate calendar for my personal life vs. stuff that affects the whole family. I created a calendar to help my extended family manage the use of a shared vacation home. I subscribe to calendars for Jewish and Christian holidays. My husband has shared his personal calendar with me. I create vacation itineraries on their own calendar. When you keep *everything* on the calendar, sometimes you need to separate the signal from the noise. Color coding approaches this on a paper calendar, but it doesn't come close to the benefit of turning off an entire category to help you focus.

This obsessive calendaring has a side benefit after the fact, too: if someone asks me when I did something, or *if* I did something, I have a reference. Too many times before I got organized, I found myself stuck with my mouth hanging open in response to a very simple question. For example: did we spend Christmas with my husband's family last year, or mine? I always think I'll remember, but I don't. Google Calendar, with its infinite history and handy search function, has saved my face more times than I can count.

AND THAT MEANS MUCH MUST NOT GO ON THE CALENDAR

Remember my friend who nearly keeled over at the sight of my calendar? When you store your whole life in there, it looks like a lot.

That means you must police your calendar strictly and protect it from anything that doesn't belong. Include everything — and I mean everything — you've committed to. Do *not* include wishful thinking.

And what's wishful thinking? Everything you hope you're going to get done. If you fill your calendar with items that don't "absolutely *have* to get done that day," writes David Allen in *Getting Things Done*, "it will dilute the emphasis on the things that truly do."

Remember how ADHD affects your brain. When it comes to prioritizing tasks and choosing (correctly and intentionally) what to do next, you're starting at a disadvantage. As Allen points out, if you have one thing that can only be done today, but you've added several less important items to your calendar, you're asking your brain to store a key piece of information: that only one of all these items is actually critical today.[25] And you've met your brain before, right?

Take a look at this section of my weekly schedule and to-do list (Figure 1). I'll talk more about the format, and why it's handwritten, in the chapter on Bullet Journaling. Note the "this week" heading at the top, where I write down the tasks I want to complete that week.

Figure 1 *Daily Log This Week*

---

25 (Allen, 2015)

This particular week contained a lot of wishful thinking (yes, I sometimes fail to follow my own advice). To-do items on this calendar page should be limited to things that become irrelevant if not done that day (or week). The items not checked off under "this week" have one thing in common: while skipping them would put me behind, I technically *could* do them the following week. This wasn't lost on my brain, and it won't be lost on yours, either.

Don't set yourself up to fail by watering down your calendar. Make sure it contains *only* items that are time-sensitive, and only on the day they are most important. Turn off any electronic calendars not directly related to your daily work and routine. For example, I keep the vacation house calendar hidden unless I'm making plans to go there and need to see if it's available. Bottom line: If you lose trust in your calendar, you'll lose your grasp on what's important today.

A NOTE ABOUT BLOCKING YOUR TIME

Many people recommend blocking out time on your calendar for specific activities. For example: paperwork from 2:00-3:30, phone calls from 10:00-10:30, and so on. I do not recommend this. If you want to trust your calendar completely, you ought to use it only for things that can only be done during the appointed time. If you clutter it with things that don't need to be there, you will make subconscious compromises with yourself.

Instead, learn to accept reality. Know and observe yourself. I know I do my best fiction writing after lunch, and that's when I try to do it. But there is no true need for me to use the time this way, and thus I know on a subconscious level that I'm not accountable for it. If I put writing on my calendar from 1:00-2:00 and something else comes up, I feel like I've failed. I also show my brain that the calendar doesn't always have the final word in my behavior. Both put continued effort and success at risk.

Of course, if I teamed up with a writing buddy to write at our desks from 1:00-2:00 and share our word counts at the end of the hour, that would go right onto the calendar. If I agree with my husband that we'll spend quality time together on Thursday night, I should put it on my calendar and hold us to it. But these are commitments I've made with other people, and thus they require an agreed-upon time. Commitments with myself are more slippery, and I am unlikely to honor them just because my calendar says so.

Perhaps you have found time blocking works for you. In this case, you likely fit the description of Rubin's rare Upholder: the consummate rule-follower for whom lists and itineraries have the final word by virtue of their very existence.

BOTTOM LINE: ASSUME YOU'LL FORGET EVERYTHING AND ACT ACCORDINGLY

When you have ADHD, nothing is too important to be forgotten. This is very difficult for people without ADHD to understand. They may fail to comprehend how your forgetfulness could *not* indicate your level of concern.

Think about your Whys here. This person, whose memory is predictable only in its unpredictability, is probably not who you want to present to the world. It's not who you want to be for the people you care about — and you should include yourself in that number, by the way. If you want to do justice to your Why, you have to stop forgetting important stuff all the time.

So go forth, and contain without shame. Just like it's okay for a person to take medication every day for a thyroid condition, it's okay for you to need more thought containers. You were born this way. If you know a way to make your life more enjoyable and structured, go on and do it. Forget what everyone else is doing, including your friend who "would die if her calendar looked like that" because she somehow remembers everything. Your needs are different, and that's okay.

Even if your thought, idea, or appointment feels unforgettable, assume you'll forget it anyway. Release your brain from its ill-fitting duty of remembering and let it shine as an idea factory. Just like the clutter in your home and office, you need to sort your mental clutter into appropriate containers before you can start down the road to an organized life.

KEY TAKEAWAYS

- If someone expects to see or hear from you at a specific time, put it on your calendar — even if your commitment was informal (e.g. "I'll think about it and get back to you next week").

- If something *can* be done on a different day, it doesn't belong on your calendar. Never include wishful thinking on your calendar.

- Kinkeeping refers to the work necessary to keep extended families connected.

- Kinkeeping obligations should be contained in your organizing system.

- Electronic solutions such as Google Calendar allow you to create separate calendars for different categories of information, which you can then hide/turn off when needed. They also accommodate recurring events and reminders.

- Assume you will forget everything, no matter how important it is.

CONTAIN INFORMATION

Let's say you've sorted through your sticky notes, synced your new Google Calendar with your phone, dumped all your unopened mail into a single basket, and started writing everything down (even the stuff you think you'll remember). As you sort the mess into containers, you'll come across a less glamorous item that nevertheless requires attention and respect: information. You probably have lots of emails, papers, and digital files that aren't flashy ideas, plans for the future, or anything actionable. Yet they hold details you may need to reference someday. They need a container, too.

Once upon a time, I enjoyed creating custom filing and storage systems. These creations gave me great satisfaction (unless I forgot my logic and couldn't find the necessary documents to file my tax return) and confounded anyone else trying to find stuff in our house. As much as I love sorting and categorizing various items, I've learned an important lesson over the years: if you live with other people, or even want to tolerate living with yourself long-term, you need to keep it simple.

Reference materials, spare buttons for your favorite pantsuit, and your child's birth certificate are all examples of things you may need infrequently, if at all. But they will cause rage and/or panic if they aren't there when you need them. Unlike the fundamentals of your daily routine — like your toothbrush or the coffeemaker — you can easily forget where they are between uses. Therefore, you should keep them somewhere simple, predictable, and accessible.

For that you'll need a good system. We'll get there in *Rule #3*. For now, as you come across these not-actionable-right-now-yet-still-important items, put them into a temporary holding container (a big plastic bin works great) with a label on it.

Why have I mentioned non-information, non-paper items in this section? Why did I include your spare buttons alongside your kid's official birth record? Because if it's small enough to fit comfortably in a hanging file folder, I'm going to suggest you keep it in one. Begin initiating your breakup with the junk drawer and the shoebox full of bits and bobs.

But in the meantime, work on collecting everything in one place. And make sure you have a filing cabinet. It doesn't have to be big. A two-drawer file cabinet is adequate for our household's spare buttons, replacement garden hose gaskets, previous years' tax returns, and everything else. Just make sure your filing container works for you and everyone else you're going to expect to use it.

USE THE CORRECT CONTAINER FOR YOUR BRAIN

Are you a visual thinker? Do you have one in your midst? Be mindful of your choice of filing cabinet. If you don't yet own a filing cabinet, great! This means you can give careful thought to what you need before making a purchase.

Before you get to *Rule #3*, you'll need to acquire a place to store important files and itty-bitties like those pantsuit buttons. Spoiler alert: I'm going to insist on something that stores those hanging folders with the little metal ears on either side. I love traditional filing cabinets for myself, but I've met visual thinkers with ADHD who literally cannot use them. For these people, a filing rack, which keeps hanging files visible all the time, can make the difference between using a filing system and stashing everything in teetering piles. For everything opaque in the office — filing cabinets, three-ring binders, file folders — there is a transparent equivalent.

GO SMALL, AND EXPAND ONLY IF NECESSARY

If you're shopping for a new file cabinet, err on the side of smaller, rather than something large enough to contain everything you have right now. I've yet to meet someone who has ADHD and loves paper filing. Most of us won't revisit these files on a regular basis to eliminate the unnecessary and obsolete, either. Between switching to digital copies for many of your paper records and getting rid of the junk, you'll probably find yourself needing less storage space than you would if you filed everything you have right now.

If you have a huge filing backlog, I still recommend shooting for a standard two-drawer file cabinet. If you're already mostly digital and have relatively little paper floating around your house, you may only need a single file crate or rolling file rack.

A NOTE ABOUT DIGITAL VS. PAPER RECORD-KEEPING

You'll meet purists on both sides: people who insist we should keep no paper records, and people who suggest filing everything in its physical form, preferably in a bomb shelter in your backyard. The reality for our ADHD household is, we want physical copies of certain things. We also aren't willing to spend a lot of time maintaining paper files. Like most situations in life, the ideal solution lies somewhere in the middle.

When we reach *Rule #3*, I'll talk more about managing digital and paper files. I'll explain why I recommend scanning and shredding whatever you can. For now, prepare to contain in a digital format some of the information you currently have on paper.

This digitizing process will be tedious, and your ADHD brain will try to keep you from sitting down to do it. You'll want to make it as easy as possible with the right scanner for the job. My favorite solution is a compact duplex document scanner. Its automatic feed and ability to scan two-sided pages make it the best choice for everyday filing tasks. We have a Brother model that has held up well for several years. If you can spend $100-$150 on a scanner, consider picking one of these up. It will make your life, and your inbox, a much tidier place. If you can't afford a new piece of equipment right now, apps like Genius Scan can convert a photo from your smart phone's camera to a PDF document.

Our family also owns a high-resolution flatbed scanner. This scanner works well for photos and negatives as well as anything oversized — or paper with popsicle sticks and buttons glued to it. In other words, parents of small children may want a flatbed scanner to archive art projects that aren't strictly paper. People with large quantities of photos on film may want a negative scanner. If you don't want to invest the money or space in a flatbed scanner (ours takes up around 11 x 19 inches of desk space and sells for over $200), you can find a reputable negative scanning service or try a smart phone app like Keepy or Artkive to preserve children's art.

KEY TAKEAWAYS

- Don't worry about catching up on your filing yet, but prepare for *Rule #3* by making sure you have a filing cabinet and scanner ready to go.

- Make sure your filing cabinet suits your needs and your brain.

- Look for a scanner that will make it easy to save your most common types of documents and pictures.

CONTAIN THOSE LOOSE ENDS

It was quite possibly the worst meeting I've ever attended. Our team sat down on a Monday morning to debrief on the recent relaunch of our company's website. It was the culmination of months of work, but no one was there to celebrate.

My colleagues' conversation around the conference table quickly erupted into open hostility. One friend and coworker displayed such open contempt and disrespect, I never looked at our interactions the same way again. I found myself wishing I'd never seen this side of the people whose company I had so enjoyed.

The worst part: I could have prevented it. All of it.

Half of our team thought the website's content wasn't ready. I agreed. The problem was, I'd sent frequent reminders over the past several weeks asking each department to polish and update their sections. I'd created a spreadsheet to log each task along with the deadline and the person responsible for completing it. And everyone seemed to have something better to do. Unwilling to miss my deadline because no one else could be bothered to so much as respond to an email, I went live with the content I had. If they'd wanted something else, surely they would've at least made a token effort.

I'd gotten into trouble this way before, but never when the stakes were so high. You see, I believed that once I sent an email, it was the other person's job to read it and respond appropriately. I certainly felt responsible for everything that came into my inbox, and I'd apologized for my own email-related oversights in the past. When I sent an email asking someone for something, I let my brain forget about it. The email was out of sight, out of mind. Not my problem. Except when a website went live with unapproved content, it was my problem — regardless of what happened in someone else's inbox.

"I never read that email," my colleagues said, even though I'd sent many. I'd even copied my boss. But that wasn't good enough for such an important project. Did the other members of the team screw up? Should they have managed their email inboxes more effectively and taken my repeated requests, reminders, and deadline updates more seriously? Of course. But at the end of the day, it was my project. I needed to keep tabs on my open loops, and I failed.

LEADING IS TAKING RESPONSIBILITY

This website launch debacle was especially disheartening to me because it violated a core management principle I'd carried with me since my very first day of gainful employment, at age 14. When I started work as an assistant in my uncle's cabinetry shop, he revealed to me the secret to all the promotions he received before founding his own shop. "Whenever anything went wrong, I took the blame!" he said. "Even if some other guy had screwed up, I'd raise my hand and say, 'Sorry, my bad.'"

This has stayed in the front of my mind ever since. Professionally, it keeps me focused on problems and solutions, not people and behaviors. I've never hesitated to take responsibility for organizational failures, or seek out opportunities for improvement. A good friend and former boss once referred to my "constant quest for self-improvement" as a trait that set me apart from others.

At home, this mindset keeps me from blaming or shaming members of my household for messes, meltdowns, and screw-ups. This is critical when you live with ADHD, either in yourself or in your family. ADHD can make you feel powerless to change or improve your situation. Always viewing yourself as a leader with agency and power will help you identify small ways you can gain a foothold, even when the deck feels stacked against you.

This isn't to say I take the blame for everything or hesitate to hold others accountable. Quite the contrary. If I demonstrate the confidence to own my role in a bad situation, I find it makes others feel more comfortable backing down and doing the same.

I felt angry and disappointed with my colleagues for their lack of follow-through and poor prioritization on the website project, but I harbored no grudges. Looking back, I see it as a big lesson about leading teams and following up on loose ends.

These loose ends, the places where we're waiting for another person to do something before we can proceed, offer us an opportunity to shine — as long as we don't drop the ball. In the office or at home, your ability to keep track of what you expect from others — and follow up until you get it — will define your success and earn you major respect.

To that end, you must collect each and every loose end in a proper container where you can easily see a list of items you're waiting on from other people.

EMAIL: THE LOOSE END GENERATING MACHINE

Email has become the default business communication tool for almost everyone. I use it for most of my personal communications as well. Unlike text messages or social media, email allows me to sort and archive messages into categories, just like I would store a piece of paper in a hanging file folder. Email software also offers a search function that can help me find information in seconds. And yet the speed at which we can fire off emails asking people for this and that can lead to a staggering number of loose ends.

Whenever you hit Send on an email that requires a response, make sure you somehow tag that message as unresolved. You need a container for emails that may require follow-up. They cannot simply float to their final resting place in your Sent folder.

There are a few ways to do this. Whichever email system you use, it probably offers labels and/or folders to sort and archive your messages. Folders mimic a physical filing cabinet, where messages can be dragged to a single folder. With labels, you may apply as many as you like to a single message. No matter which you use, set up a tag or folder titled Waiting or something similar. In *Getting Things Done*, David Allen suggests adding the @ symbol to the beginning of your Waiting label to make sure it stays at the top of your folder/label list.[26]

If your email program uses only folders to organize messages, I recommend adding yourself to the cc: or bcc: line on any outgoing message where you've asked someone to do something. A supervisor recommended this to me years ago, and it was a lifesaver. When the message arrives in your inbox, drag it to your @Waiting folder.

---

26 (Allen, 2015)

Labels, a popular Gmail feature, allow you to skip this step. When composing a message, I apply my @Waiting label before I even click Send. No need to add myself to the recipient list. The message is automatically stored under the @Waiting label as soon as I send it.

Whatever method you choose, make sure you have a single, easy-to-access spot where you can view all emails containing outstanding requests.

MANAGING LOOSE ENDS IN THE REAL WORLD

Like my inboxes, I keep my loose-end containers to a bare minimum. There are situations — emergency rooms are a good example — where people with ADHD excel at keeping a lot of balls in the air. Many people with ADHD work in emergency medicine for that reason: we thrive on the constant stimulation and stress.

You do not want your everyday life to operate this way. When it comes to the daily grind, keeping too many balls in the air is a surefire way to drop one. Given the distraction and forgetfulness so common in people with ADHD, you'll do well to keep your system as simple and centralized as possible.

I keep my loose ends, the items where I've left the ball in someone else's court, in one of only three places. Aside from my email, I keep a physical folder of things I'm waiting on, or some receive a Waiting status in my task management app.

Loose Ends in a To-Do App

Some people choose to use a 100-percent physical system to stay on top of their projects and tasks. You can certainly accomplish this with an array of file folders, notebooks, legal pads, tickler files, and the like. I'm often on the go and like to have access to my projects and tasks from anywhere in the world. I also dislike too much physical clutter. It's much more difficult to rummage through a stack of papers than to perform a quick search in an app. While I store a substantial amount of information in my office filing cabinet, I manage as much as possible electronically.

The meat of my project and to-do list management lives in an app called Toodledo. The basic version of Toodledo, which contains all the features I need, is free and contains no advertisements. It meets my core criteria of possessing all the features necessary to implement GTD. This includes tags to mark a task's status. One of these status tags is *Waiting*.

One of the most convenient aspects of a project management app like Toodledo is the ability to change a task's status from *Next Action* — something on my plate — to Waiting with a single mouse click. Each week, I click on this Waiting status to review the outstanding items in all my projects, all in one place.

Toodledo isn't the only app of its kind on the market, but as of this writing, it's the best I've found to integrate all aspects of GTD in one place. If you choose another system, just make sure you create a separate container for loose ends. Don't let them slip away.

Loose Ends in a Physical Folder

Of course, not all Waiting items come from tasks in my Toodledo app. When I write a check, I hold onto the carbon copy until it clears. Sometimes I call a customer service line with questions about a bill or bank statement. I keep a record of our conversation by writing notes on the document itself — including information about when I expect to receive a call back. I store these items in a folder in the front of my desk's file drawer. This also makes it convenient to drop documents and sticky notes into the folder as I process my inbox or make phone calls at my desk. At the beginning of the week I pull the folder out and look at each item, following up as needed.

LOOSE ENDS CONNECT YOU TO THE REST OF THE WORLD

Of all the strategies I use to keep my life organized, my Waiting lists seem to have the biggest effect on how other people perceive me. They serve as the public face of my adult responsibilities. When a promised email doesn't arrive, I'm the person who asks after it. Many times, I've helped others avoid a crisis simply by circling back and asking, "Where did we land on this?" I can't count the number of times someone has said to me, "Thank goodness you're so organized."

Some of you may be thinking, *Wait, I thought she said we weren't getting organized for other people. I thought I wasn't supposed to care what other people think. I'm supposed to be doing this for myself.*

True. But think back to your Why. How might your Why be supported if you took responsibility, or even took the lead, more often? If you didn't let opportunities pass you by while you waited for someone to find time to get back to you? Consider this example from my life:

Every fall, I spend a weekend with my college friends. We began as four friends, three of whom lived together and one of whom we called an honorary roommate. Our ranks have grown over the years as we've added spouses and children. The group now includes seven adults and six children hailing from four cities across three states. Getting everyone in one place for an entire weekend every year is no small feat! I start pinging people over the summer to nail down our date for the fall.

How have I become the de facto leader of this group? Why do they give me credit for making the whole thing come together every year? It's not just because I write it down as a project in my list. If I did that, a year would pass us by. I'd shrug and say, "It's too hard to even get people to respond to an email asking when they're available, let alone plan a time and place for us all to get together!"

Containing our loose ends in a place where we can easily find them and spot potential problems is the most critical element of our interactions with others. It's what separates those who have lots of good ideas from those who actually make them happen.

I'm known among my family and friends as the person who makes vacation and project plans happen. It's not because I know how to get a response from people. I still haven't figured out how to write an email everyone will read and respond to the first time. They never do. What sets me apart is my ability to keep an eye on those non-responses and follow up, on a weekly basis and across several channels if necessary, until I have everything I need to take the next step.

This skill — gathering and storing your loose ends effectively — will help you both personally and professionally. Without the ability to stay on top of outstanding requests, you'll find yourself missing out on opportunities and operating in crisis mode more than you'd like.

KEY TAKEAWAYS

- Your ability to follow up on loose ends and outstanding requests can define you both personally and professionally.

- Sending an email or leaving a voicemail asking someone for something is not enough. If you don't hear back, you are responsible for staying on top of your request.

- Whenever you make a request, store that request in a container/file with other loose ends. Always make a record of what you expect from other people and when you expect it.

CONTAIN SOURCES OF DISTRACTION AND INAPPROPRIATE HYPERFOCUS

While the first D in ADHD stands for *deficit*, people with ADHD don't start out with less attention than everyone else. ADHD cripples our attention *regulation*, stripping us of the choice as to where our attention focuses — or doesn't. As you sweep your chaos into containers, you'll do well to consider which tangible and intangible items cause you to hit a snag.

People with ADHD can be derailed by too many distractions, like cell phone notifications beeping every 90 seconds. We also fall victim to the opposite: tunnel vision that removes us from time and reality. Judging from the ubiquity of the "look! a squirrel!" cliché, most people know all about ADHD and distraction. You may not know about its counterpart, hyperfocus. Both hyperfocus and distraction can ruin your day. Identify and contain sources of both.

Full disclosure: I harbor a tiny bit of anti-hyperfocus bias. I experience it less often than some ADHDers, which makes me disinclined to laud it as an ADHD superpower. When I do hyperfocus, it often manifests in a negative emotional state that I wish I could escape.

My husband, on the other hand, is a champion hyperfocuser. While this gives him stamina to pull all-nighters when the need arises, it also gives him stamina to pull all-nighters when the need has *not* arisen — and I'm expecting him to share half of a long drive the next day. If hyperfocus is a superpower, it must be trained and managed. Left unchecked, it does far more harm than good.

SO, WHAT IS HYPERFOCUS?

As I've mentioned elsewhere, viewing ADHD as an *attention deficit* misses the point. Plenty of people with ADHD have no trouble turning on obsessive laser focus and spending hours on a single task — provided it's something that engages their interest. This is hyperfocus.[27]

I've heard several people with ADHD describe hyperfocus as a state where *time actually ceases to exist*. This is the problem with traditional hyperfocus-related advice to look at a clock more often, wear a watch, or set a timer. The hyperfocus state means more than simply losing track of time. Its victim forgets time exists at all, until it's too late. Even a timer, if it fails to intrude enough to break the mental spell, can be easily silenced and forgotten.

Breaking the hyperfocus flow feels *bad*. If you've ever tried to disengage a person with ADHD from something they really, really wanted to keep doing, and you've been met with disproportionate hostility or downright childishness, you've seen what I'm talking about. If that doesn't resonate, you may want to search your own life for times when you struggle to stop what you're doing.

I discovered a major source of hyperfocus empathy in an unexpected place: my sewing table. As I hit my late 20s, I found myself with some custom home décor needs. I'd also been treating my ADHD for a few years. I decided to take up sewing, an activity I'd previously shunned because it required too much patience. It went surprisingly well, and I kept learning new skills and taking on increasingly challenging projects.

As I worked, I noticed something happening in my brain. I got into the zone with sewing in a way I usually found impossible. I'd finish a seam and want to sew up one more raw edge, and then one more. As the finished product grew nearer, I found it harder to put it down. Sometimes I'd work on a project for several hours, even if I wasn't particularly enjoying it.

I mentioned this to my husband, who writes computer software by trade and as a hobby. That's exactly what software engineering is, he told me, except there's *always* one more raw edge. The project can go on forever.

---

27 (Hinshaw & Ellison, 2016)

This kind of thing can become an addiction for a person with ADHD — especially one who struggles with controlling hyperfocus and switching tasks. The reason? A little neurotransmitter called dopamine.

DOPAMINE: THE ROOT OF OUR DESIRE

To understand hyperfocus, not to mention ADHD in general, we must first understand dopamine's role in our brains and our behavior. Dopamine fuels our brain's reward system. It helps us control what we pay attention to, how we respond to stimuli, and how we corral our behavior in service of a goal.[28] Many professionals and lay people describe ADHD as a dopamine deficiency, but this doesn't tell the whole story. ADHD can't be defined numerically, in terms of a measured shortage of dopamine in the brain.[29] However, we do know people with ADHD have less dopamine available and at our service.[30] This limitation causes some of ADHD's most baffling behaviors.

If you still think people with ADHD must be, at some level, making a choice to avoid responsibilities and spend hours buried in a meaningless project, consider some of these studies done on rats:

When researchers implant rats' brains with electrodes to stimulate the reward system, the rats will stop at nothing to keep the dopamine hits coming. Rats have run across electrified grids to press stimulation triggers until their feet became too charred to continue. And yet, if you destroy this area of the brain, something even more fascinating will happen: a rat will still experience pleasure if you reward it with a sugar cube, but it will no longer work for that reward. Dopamine controls something deeper than pleasure and stimulation. It controls our cravings and desires.[31]

With too little available dopamine, we can still experience a pleasurable reward, but we don't crave it before we have it. Our logical brain knows we *should* want it, but the part that drives us to work for it is out to lunch.

This has tremendous implications for people with ADHD. It explains why stimulant medications, which increase the amount of dopamine available in the brain, can have such a dramatic effect. It also explains why someone might know what they need to do, but repeatedly fail to do it. And it explains why a person with ADHD will hyperfocus on an activity that provides repeated dopamine boosts.

---

28 (McGonigal, 2012)
29 (Pera, 2008)
30 (Barkley, 2010)
31 (McGonigal, 2012)

Remember, dopamine is all about the *promise* of a reward. We'll binge on junk food even if we don't really enjoy it. Its high fat and sugar content gives us a dopamine hit. Same with scrolling through Facebook, which is engineered to manipulate your brain's reward system and keep you staring at your news feed. Video games can provide such an intense dopamine rush, the crash upon stopping the game can intensify ADHD symptoms.[32] Remember my conversation with my husband about sewing and computer programming? How there's always another raw edge? I'll leave you to guess what's happening in our brains every time we sense an opportunity to sew one up.

IF YOU'RE HELPING SOMEONE ELSE...

Because I'm more prone to distraction than hyperfocus, I've had to work hard to empathize with my husband, who's just the opposite. My experience with the sewing machine was a huge breakthrough for us because I finally understood what he was talking about: the sensation of knowing you should stop, yet being unable to. People without ADHD, especially those with naturally excellent self-control, may lack any concept of how this could *not* be a choice. Either I'm choosing to be responsible, or I'm choosing to be irresponsible. End of story.

It's not that simple. As frustrating as hyperfocus can be when your spouse gets wrapped up in something and neglects food, sleep, and family, it helps to remind yourself she's not actually making a conscious choice. She hasn't said to herself, "Continuing this activity is more important than my family." He doesn't decide at 9:00 p.m., "I think I'll stay up until 4:00 a.m. playing World of Warcraft." In fact, before you even say a word to us, we've usually beat ourselves up internally. We know we did you wrong, and we wanted to do better, we just…didn't. And we're as frustrated about that as you are.

It may help to view conversations about this behavior as though you're speaking to an addict. In a way, you are! Those dopamine rewards for making a piece of your software work, or beating a video game boss, or sewing up a raw edge, affect the brain similarly to some hard drugs. If your loved one doesn't have his ADHD under control with a solid treatment plan—probably including stimulant medication—these hyperfocus activities may provide his sole experience of desire for, and effective progress toward, a goal. If he feels you are trying to take that feeling away, you're in for a battle.

For people who struggle to focus on undesirable tasks all day, letting the brain run wild can also be an intense relief. "Someone else owns my time all day," my husband once told me. When he came home from work, he wanted to relax. He certainly didn't want me telling him what to do.

I know how this must sound, but don't lose hope quite yet. Because hyperfocus is all about

---

32 (Pera, 2015)

rewards and self-regulation, proper treatment of ADHD's underlying neurochemical imbalances will help a lot. Rather than screaming about this specific behavior, focus on getting your loved one on an effective treatment plan. Reread the first section of this book, and know that without good symptom management, trying to control hyperfocus is like swimming against a riptide.

FINDING YOUR HYPERFOCUS SWEET SPOT

Of course, as troublesome as it can be, hyperfocus isn't *all* bad. It shares many characteristics with a state described as *flow*, where we find ourselves absorbed in the moment, unaware of the passage of time, focused solely on the task in front of us.[33]

All the same, you need to learn to harness your hyperfocus. You can declutter your home, get every appointment and obligation onto your calendar, and set up an airtight system for capturing your tasks and loose ends. Yet it means nothing without some control over your minute-to-minute behavior. Having a calendar that accurately depicts the landscape of your day is only step one. If you then get so wrapped up in what you're doing that you forget to eat, look at a clock, or reference that calendar until 4:00 p.m., you do not have your life in order.

HYPERFOCUS CORRALS

In *Better Than Before*, Gretchen Rubin insists we must "decide not to decide."[34] In other words, skip the part where you must choose to do the right thing. Decide ahead of time, and work on autopilot as much as possible.

People with ADHD, who struggle with self-regulation and making the right choice in the moment, would do well to heed this advice. Return to the concepts from this book's *Know Thyself* chapter and make a list of your hyperfocus triggers. How can you contain these triggers so you don't waste mental energy resisting them at every turn?

Here are just a few ways to limit hyperfocus temptations:

---

33 (Nakamura & Csikszentmihalyi, 2009)
34 (Rubin, 2015)

Set Boundaries Ahead of Time and Commit to Sticking to Them

Practically speaking, you probably can't remove all temptation and vulnerability from your life. Nor should you. For many people with ADHD, hyperfocus may be inextricably linked to your career or personal passions. However, even the most noble pursuits should not negatively impact your heath, family, or relationships.

Know your brain and know when you're vulnerable to hyperfocus. Perhaps you need to create a rule for yourself that you will not use your computer after 9:30 p.m., or you will not start watching a new episode of a TV show within one hour of your bedtime.

For screen-related temptations, there are several apps on the market to help you focus on the task at hand — and not on a three-hour Wikipedia or YouTube rabbit hole. The popular Freedom app for Mac, Windows, and iOS allows you to restrict access to distracting apps and websites during time slots of your choice. I use an extension called Productivity Owl for Google's Chrome browser to guide my online behavior. The owl allows me to spend only an allotted amount of time on any given website (my setting is five minutes) before it swoops in and closes the browser tab. Of course, it provides the option to set exceptions (sites with no time limit) as well as block certain sites altogether. I can also control when the owl is watching and when it gives me a break.

If you keep hyperfocus traps in your bedroom, remove them. If you've ever fought with your spouse (or yourself) over sleep or sex, I don't need to tell you why. I've even had to bar myself from reading certain books in bed, lest I accidentally stay up all night reading them. Behind every five-star rating on my Goodreads list lurks several hours of missed sleep.

Consider carefully where you engage in hyperfocus activities in your home or office. Do you want to be available for your family when you're in the living room or sitting at the dining room table? Then perhaps you should limit the number of hyperfocus opportunities in these areas, rather than find yourself frustrated or even hostile when the inevitable interruptions occur.

Besides sewing, which I do alone in the basement, my other hyperfocus jam is reading. When you interrupt me in the middle of reading a novel, you may as well be waking me from a deep sleep and expecting me to listen with enthusiasm and attentiveness. Consequently, I almost never read books in situations where I know I'll be interrupted. Sitting at the dining room table or on the living room couch, you'll find me reading magazine articles, which don't trigger my hyperfocus and which I'm happy to look away from if needed.

These suggestions will work better for some than others. For people who feel a natural repulsion to rules and order, most boundaries will feel arbitrary. If you're afraid this might be you, return to your Why. Connect these boundaries deeply to your purpose for organizing. What are you making room for by corralling inappropriate moments of hyperfocus? Where will you spend that extra time? For whom do you want to be more present? If you need to, create physical reminders to keep your Why front and center at times when you think you're most likely to hyperfocus.

Ask for Help

Make agreements with family, colleagues, or helpful friends. Tell them to be persistent even if you resist, make excuses, or tell them to go to the meeting and you'll be right behind them. Agree ahead of time that this is unacceptable behavior and ask them to remind you whenever necessary.

Also, remember that you've asked this person for their help and support because you're struggling with self-regulation. Try to listen, cooperate, and be gracious.

Engage the Senses

A hyperfocusing person may not remember a conversation that occurs during their hyperfocus, and they may not even notice anything happening around them.

Because hyperfocus takes us so deep into the zone, we often need more than a simple, "Time to leave for dinner—now." A sensory event can help with transitions and bring your consciousness back to the real world. Ask others to turn the lights off, provide a gentle touch on the arm or shoulder, or set a timer with a loud bell and place it across the room.

The growing market of smart home technology makes it easy to do this for yourself. We have a smart light bulb in our living room lamp that turns off at 11:00 p.m. on weeknights. When the room goes dark, it suddenly feels inappropriate to continue our usual activities. More often than not, we go to bed when the light goes out. An old-fashioned lamp timer works as well. If you want to get fancy, you can program smart switches to dim the lights or shut off your television's power outlet at a specific hour.

IN CASE OF EMERGENCY: HYPERFOCUS RESCUE REMEDY

I'm going to talk straight to people *helping* a person with ADHD here because people stuck under the hyperfocus spell often lack the self-awareness to break it. They need your help.

Try this simple trick: ask the person to close their eyes and imagine themselves at some point in the future. Make it mundane. I've imagined myself standing in the kitchen preparing dinner. I've asked my son to visualize himself walking from the house to the car on his way to school in the morning. The moment can be ordinary and should be unrelated to the current hyperfocus state.

I know it sounds strange, but it works. I discovered this strategy, which I later found articulated in Kelly McGonigal's *The Willpower Instinct*, while deep in the depths of a negative emotional hyperfocus. (Yes, hyperfocus can apply to emotions, too, leaving you with no grasp on anything outside what you are currently feeling. And yes, this can be dangerous. People with ADHD are at a nearly fivefold risk for self-harm.[35])

Following a disagreement with my husband, I found myself unable to let go. It was late. He wanted to go to bed. The disagreement wasn't a big deal, but it felt unresolved. My emotions spiraled out of control until I'd lost all perspective. I knew imposing my emotional state on my husband would only stir up drama, so I left the room to calm down by myself.

Except I didn't calm down. I convinced myself my family would be better off without me and I would never contribute anything of value to the world. I cried uncontrollably and felt terribly alone. Desperate for a lifeline, I closed my eyes and pictured myself in the middle of my kitchen. It was a normal weekend afternoon. I was cooking food for family and friends, surrounded by people whose company I enjoyed. I tried to place myself there in as much detail as possible.

As my brain grabbed onto that scene, I felt like a fog was lifting. The rest of the world, and my life at large, reappeared and felt real once again.

Our brains have different regions for thinking about ourselves and about other people. When you stay up too late or order that one last drink and think, "I'm going to regret this tomorrow," your brain uses the brain regions dedicated to thinking about *other people*.[36] We don't connect to our future self as deeply as our present self. That's why your hyperfocusing ADHDer won't pull themselves away from the video game to mow the lawn. The person who will be in trouble for not mowing the lawn *feels like someone else*.

Imagining a moment in the future, even if it's something as simple as a trip to the grocery store, helps us connect to ourselves outside the moment.[37] Use this to your advantage when you're trying to help someone break their hyperfocus. Just make sure you're coming from a genuinely helpful place and not offering a scolding, "I want you to think about how tired you're going to be tomorrow if you don't get to bed." It will help to discuss this strategy beforehand and allow your loved one to accept your assistance. Someone who views you, not the hyperfocus state, as the primary problem is unlikely to cooperate no matter how many brain science tricks you throw at them.

---

35 (Paul, 2015, July 20)
36 (McGonigal, 2012)
37 (McGonigal, 2012)

BOTTOM LINE: SERVE YOUR WHY

People with ADHD crave hyperfocus. In the right context it can feel productive or, at the very least, like a nice break from trying to corral our attention. Usually, our hyperfocus is fed by a stream of small rewards. We gain experience or win battles in video games. We sew another seam. We fix another bug in the software.

The problem arises when this hyperfocus gets in the way of our Why. You may finally finish that big project that had you holed up in the basement all weekend, only to find your spouse unable to share your pride. He may feel abandoned and unappreciated because you left him to wrangle the kids and cook all the meals, and he's hardly seen you. Perhaps you reached the highest level in your favorite online role-playing game, but failed to do laundry and now have no clean clothes for work tomorrow. Maybe you wish you had more of a social life, yet don't have time for the basics of caring for your home and family. You don't even know where the time goes.

When we don't choose its direction and duration, our hyperfocus can betray us. It can steal time without our even being aware of its passing. This is time you can use to put your life in order and enjoy deeper connections with your friends and family. Don't let it get away from you.

CONTAIN YOUR DISTRACTIONS, TOO

If you have trouble relating to hyperfocus issues, you may inhabit my end of the ADHD spectrum. While I may disappear into a time warp while reading a good book, the sad reality is that I struggle to pay attention to anything long enough for it to matter. I need to police and contain my distractions more than my hyperfocus.

Remember the Productivity Owl browser extension I use? Sometimes it swoops in to close a browser tab and I realize I have no idea what I was doing on that website. I have no choice but to go back to the last thing I was doing and hope I didn't forget anything too important.

A deeper reflection on your learning styles may give you hints as to which distractions will prove most crippling for you. My husband, a visual thinker, struggles to tune out sounds while he's working. This, combined with the ADHD brain's already-weak distraction filter, makes working in an open office with cubicles challenging for him. He says he "can't not listen" to conversations happening around him. Sometimes he uses headphones to listen to music, but that can hurt his focus, too. He finally found success in a CD with various kinds of static noise, which he plays through his headphones.

This is a good example of an environment you cannot control. Relatively few people working outside the home have the luxury of a private office anymore. A friend's employer did away with cubicles in favor of shared tables or working on a laptop in the company cafeteria. Much has been written on both sides of the debate between closed and open office plans. I won't discuss it here except to say that as a person with ADHD, you may be expected to work in an environment that actively undermines your focus.

Your physical environment at work cannot, however, be an excuse for disorganization and poor productivity. If you can, ask for a cubicle away from main thoroughfares or even in a back corner. If you're stuck in a distraction zone, do whatever you can to control your environment and contain those distractions — or, more accurately, to contain yourself from them. Headphones with white noise, nature sounds, or music can help a lot.

If You're a Full-Time Caregiver, You're Not "Just" Anything

These days, it's easy to think a stay-at-home parent is *just staying home with the children*. What excuse could a full-time mom or dad have for being totally disorganized?

First of all, you aren't "just" anything. As a stay-at-home parent, I take primary responsibility for child care as well as the house. Many administrative responsibilities fall on me, not to mention keeping our home clean and organized.

This doesn't come easily for many adults with ADHD. Young children create a wealth of distractions. If yours aren't yet school-aged, you may find yourself wondering where your time goes. Children add noise, interruptions, and clutter to your environment. Meanwhile, you must make time for paying bills, making phone calls, organizing your calendar, and doing housework.

If you're handling bills, communications with repair people, family correspondence, and the like, you need a place to do this that works for your brain. I've insisted upon a dedicated office in our home with a door that closes. This may not be possible for everyone. Carve out the best space you can. Give yourself a desk, a place to sit that signals, "I'm working now." Don't try to organize your life from the dining room table while your kids run circles around it. At least wait until they're asleep or watching a movie. You have a real and important role to play in your family. You deserve a place to do this work, even if it's a glorified closet or a neglected corner of the guest bedroom.

Smart Phones: Distraction's Best Friend

I depend on my smart phone, but I do not love it. I can spend a long time tapping around while never remembering the reason I picked it up in the first place. Smart phones provide an unparalleled toolbox of ADHD supports, but they bring just as many distractions.

My methods for containing these distractions may feel uncomfortable to you at first, especially if you're a heavy smart phone user. Some people depend so heavily on their smart phones that they experience significant separation anxiety when the phone isn't there.[38]

I think of smart phones a little like sugar. Have you ever done a 30-day sugar detox? The beginning can be pretty rocky. While I avoid extreme diets even in the short term, I do try to limit my refined sugar consumption to almost zero. I've found that this has not only decreased my cravings for sweets, I actually find most sugary snacks and drinks unappealing.

In the same way, I've found the less time I spend with a smart phone within arm's reach, the less interested I am in using it — and the less it distracts me. But I need to contain it, or else it will take over my life.

What Is Your Smart Phone Actually *For*?

Before you start organizing your phone to contain those distractions, ask yourself: why do I have this device? What purpose does it serve in my life?

This goes back to your Why: the kind of person you want to be for yourself and others. I use my smart phone to stay organized and keep in touch with family and friends. My phone makes a lot of this stuff easier and more efficient. For example, I can review my calendar at any time. Whether I'm leaving my doctor's office and need to schedule an appointment or chatting with a friend about grabbing lunch, I can check availability and put the date on my calendar then and there. If I forget to bring a document to a meeting, I can pull it up on my phone using Dropbox (a file-syncing app). The smart phone's ability to sync massive amounts of information to the cloud gives me access to almost anything I need wherever I go.

However, the smart phone's limitless possibilities can also lead to a lot of wasted time. Consider your Why and ask yourself for each app, "Is this something I really need or want to do *on my phone*?"

---

38 (Cheever, 2014)

Games are a good example. I enjoy games, but now limit myself to tabletop gaming and dedicated game consoles such as the PlayStation or Xbox. Phone games offer up too much temptation to fritter away time I could be using for something else. Likewise with Facebook, which many people use to stay in touch with friends and family. While I will visit the website on my computer, I do not keep the app on my phone.

I use my phone for what it does best: playing music and podcasts, navigating me to unfamiliar destinations, maintaining my calendar, quickly checking email, taking photos, sending short messages, and using a few language learning apps. If an activity can be done better on a computer or other device, I try to avoid it on my phone.

In other words, if you want your smart phone to work for you, you need to organize your apps. Ruthlessly eliminate anything that undermines your Why, just as you would declutter a physical room in your house. Your phone is an electronic Swiss Army knife. Notice that there are many models of Swiss Army knife because everyone wants a slightly different combination of tools. It wouldn't do to carry a knife with every available tool attached, nor should you install every app you enjoy or think you might use. There is not room, in your day or in your brain, for everything.

Notifications and Home Screens: The First Line of Defense When the Phone Is in Your Hand

Notifications are those little banners that appear at the top of your screen, or the little red number in the corner of an app icon. On Android phones, some notifications change the color of the phone's blinking LED. Other apps provide a preview of the notification's contents on the phone's lock screen.

All of these are intended to make you look at your phone. If you're anything like me, five other things will catch your eye as soon as you pick it up. You may not even make it to the app that originally begged for your attention.

Here's my advice: view your notifications like an inbox. Aim for as few as possible. Minimize the number of apps that can provide notifications at all. I have a few social media apps that I check daily. I don't allow them to notify me proactively of anything except for direct messages, when someone is speaking to me one-on-one. Instead of asking yourself to justify turning off an app's notifications, force yourself to justify keeping each notification turned *on*.

Likewise, make sure the remaining notifications alert you in a way that is appropriate and respectful. You wouldn't want someone sitting next to you to interrupt you every time something new crossed their mind. Don't accept that behavior from your phone, either. I've silenced all notifications except for the actual phone ringing. Many notifications still vibrate, but none cause my phone to engage in disruptive or distracting behavior.

By now, perhaps I've triggered your fear of missing out. Trust me: any notification on your phone can wait. You will remember to pick up your phone from time to time to check for new messages. If you keep your ringer enabled, people can reach you in an emergency.

Once you pick up your phone, make sure the first thing you see offers minimal distractions and maximum utility. Android phones allow users to customize the appearance of the phone's home screen quite extensively. Mine displays only two large widgets: one with the weather, another with the day's calendar. My text messaging, camera, and web browser apps occupy a row of icons along the bottom of the screen. When I'm just checking a notification or sending a quick text, this is all I see — no social media, no news. Subsequent home screens offer more tools, curated based on frequency of use.

Even if you cannot create a 100 percent customized experience, all smart phones allow the user to rearrange apps on the home screen(s). Think twice about including social media apps on the first screen you see when unlocking your phone. Stay away from anything that might distract you or suck you in with a promise of new information. If you must include social media on your home screen, try disabling those little red badge numbers in the corner of the app icon.

Here are sample home screens from an iPhone and an Android phone. Notice how the iPhone home screen (Figure 2) includes more items but still lacks social media apps with tempting news feeds (e.g. Twitter, Instagram, Facebook). App icons are also displayed singly, not in cluttered folders on the home screen. The Android operating system (Figure 3) allows more customization with large, transparent widgets for a more minimalist view.

Figure 2 *iPhone Home Screen*

Figure 3 *Android Home Screen*

Bottom line: your phone offers many distractions. Without your intervention, your phone will hurt your efforts to get organized more than it will help. You need to recognize those distractions and contain them away from your immediate view.

Literal Phone Containment

Consider assigning a home for cell phones to help set expectations for phone use and family interactions. A small basket or bin labeled "cell phones" may even inspire guests to deposit their phones when visiting your home. I keep a small wood bin beneath a power outlet in our kitchen. It includes three different types of phone chargers to encourage people to keep their phones there.

The act of getting up and going to the cell phone basket serves as its own barrier: I won't bother unless I have something specific to do on my phone. Though it has been subject of much eye-rolling in our home, our cell phone basket has significantly reduced the amount of time I spend aimlessly tapping around on my phone.

Not only that, a dedicated cell phone repository may help you save time previously spent looking for lost phones. If I pick up someone else's phone while tidying up, I place it in the bin. It's the first place I suggest looking when I hear, "Have you seen my phone?" It's also the storage spot for portable phone chargers. The cell phone basket, used and located wisely, provides an organized hub for smart phone use.

Turning the Smart Phone Into…A Phone

Despite the benefits of disconnecting from our phones, a complete break — even for a few hours — just isn't possible for some of us. I don't have a landline, but I do have administrative tasks that sometimes require the phone. I also have a young child in school.

At the same time, my cell phone basket has taught me to be wary of keeping my phone on my desk. My solution, and one I recommend to anyone who's given up a landline but wants some space from the smart phone, is a Bluetooth wireless system. It connects you to your phone, but at a distance.

Many landline telephone manufacturers like Panasonic and Vtech offer landline systems with Bluetooth technology. The system I have cost me less than $100 and includes a corded desk phone and two cordless phones. The corded base sits on my desk on the second floor of my house, and I keep cordless units on the first floor and in the basement. The base connects to my smart phone via Bluetooth. A call to my cell phone causes everything to ring in unison, just like the old days of landline phones. I can make or pick up a call from anywhere in my house, regardless of my cell phone's actual location. In other words, my smart phone — with all its apps and distractions — can live out of sight and out of mind for the work day without severing my connections with the outside world.

If you spend your days at home, especially if you work from a home office, and you don't have a landline, I highly recommend a system like this. It allows you to contain the distracting features of your phone while fulfilling expectations of availability for both work and family.

Give It Time

Perhaps this all sounds well and good to you, but you're thinking, "This could never fit into my life." I assure you, most of us can survive with a bit more distance from our smart phones. At first you may feel disconnected, uncomfortable, and afraid of missing out. Give it a month. Think of it like that sugar detox, where you must work through your cravings before you start to feel healthy again. Chances are you aren't the exception and you will acclimate to the reduced stimulation and distraction.

I don't spend my days cut off from the world when I'm not physically connected to my smart phone. I have a second mobile telephone number through Google's Voice service, which allows me to send and receive SMS (text) messages via Google Hangouts on my computer, and my desk telephone allows me to make and receive calls whenever I like. While referencing specific technology in a book is sure to make it feel dated within a few months, I'm confident that even as specific apps pass in and out of favor, there will remain a platform for sending and receiving text-based messages from a computer. Unless phone-based social media or mobile apps are part of your job, you don't need your smart phone during your work day.

BOTTOM LINE: STOLEN TIME LEAVES YOU IN CHAOS

This chapter may have you feeling lost in the weeds. What does all this nonsense about hyperfocus, distraction, and smart phones have to do with getting organized?

The answer is simple: when you allow your time to leak away, you end up running out of it. Have you ever had a habit of stopping for a latte on your way to work every day? When you add up the cost of that $5 daily treat over the course of a year, the effect can be quite sobering.

Like our money, we only have so much time. Also like money, mindless spending can leave us feeling strapped and helpless. If you currently feel you don't have time to get organized or you can barely keep your head above water each day before collapsing into bed hours late, you're doing the time equivalent of living paycheck to paycheck. Start collecting receipts and sketching out a budget. Add up the cost of getting sucked into a hyperfocus vortex or succumbing to distractions on your smart phone. Then, put those temptations in a box. Literally, if it comes to that. Protect your time from them, and you may find you have a little room to get organized, after all.

KEY TAKEAWAYS

- People with ADHD don't have an attention deficit, per se. They have a reduced ability to *regulate* attention.

- Hyperfocus describes an ADHDer's ability to spend hours laser-focused on a single task.

- During hyperfocus, ADHDers don't just lose track of time — it's more like time ceases to exist.

- Hyperfocusers will most likely need help learning to break the spell and transition to a new activity.

- Because ADHDers struggle to regulate attention, all distractions need to be identified and contained — preferably out of sight.

- Smart phones are great tools, but only if used wisely.

- To prevent hyperfocus and distraction from negatively impacting others, remove opportunities and temptations. Set boundaries and stick to them.

- We may have a lot more time than we think we do. Repeated small expenditures of time on things that don't serve our Why will add up.

RULE #3:
YOU NEED A SYSTEM THAT WORKS

ONCE CONTAINED, THE CHAOS MUST BECOME ORDER

It's one thing to sort and gather your life's messes into tidy containers. It's quite another to bring those containers under control and keep them that way. In one possible interpretation, I could say I contained the mess created by the Lost Room I shared with you before: I put everything in one room and freed myself to focus on the rest of the house.

I find containment relatively easy. Something sets me off, I get fed up with the mess, and I sort it all into boxes, bins, or baskets. *That's it*, I say, *the mess has to end here*. If the mess belongs to someone else, I label the box with that person's name and put it out of the way. Then I go about my life — until the mess comes back. This time, I have fewer places to hide it because I never addressed the last mess I boxed up and hid in the closet.

Once upon a time, before our basement served as a guest room, my husband had an undeniably effective strategy for cleaning up for company. Thirty to sixty minutes before our guests were to arrive, he'd go through our entire downstairs and gather all the items that didn't belong. He then shoved these items into shopping bags and put them in the basement. Remember that my husband is a visual thinker with ADHD. I'll leave you to guess how long some of those bags stayed down there.

CONTROLLING AND DIRECTING THE FLOW

Hopefully, you've contained the things that will derail your attention. You've worked on treating your ADHD to get your symptoms under control. You've assessed your personal and professional commitments and placed a high value on your time and attention. From there, you're finally in a position to start the real work.

To build an organized life, as opposed to a life with boxes of unresolved messes lurking behind closed doors, you need a system for processing what comes in. You need to keep up with the flow of emails, dirty dishes, projects, deadlines, happy hours, and family drama. You're behind right now, and you'll get behind again (In fact, as I write this, I'm behind on plenty of things, as I will always be when trying to push a book out the door). Don't worry. Once you have a system up and running, you can make time to chip away at the backlog.

Think of it like a leaky pipe. We once had one in our basement. I know what you're thinking: but all those bags of stuff you didn't want to deal with! Did they get wet? Or maybe you don't care. But I'll tell you anyway: water did get on several things I'd shoved into a corner (the one with the pipes in it) because I didn't want to deal with them.

Some people with ADHD shine in a crisis. I do, I suppose, but the crisis must be of a certain magnitude. This — a broken pipe behind our main shutoff valve — didn't make the cut. I saw water on the floor and immediately began yelling at my husband about the mess. I didn't even know what things were getting wet! Water was creeping toward the carpet! No one was getting a mop!

For the savvy reader wondering not about which things got wet, but whether anyone had the proper tool to shut off our water supply at the meter outside, congratulations. You're already on the right track. And yes, thanks to my husband and a very helpful neighbor, we did get the water turned off before anything important got ruined.

If you've amassed quite the backlog of organizing projects in your containment phase, try to ignore them for now, just like I had to ignore the puddle on the floor at first. You need to get the incoming flow under control or you'll find yourself underwater.

I'm guessing, since you're holding this book right now, that you've gotten stuck here in the past. In this section, I'm going to focus on the second half of *Rule #3*. You know you need a system, right? But many people overlook the fact that it also needs to *work*. You need a system *that works*. For you.

Before we look at the nitty gritty, let's take a giant step backward and remember what we've learned thus far. Whatever you do, don't leap into a new system before considering the realities of your life and your brain. People with ADHD will not follow an organizational system for its own sake. We need a Why, and we need to tailor our system to our unique brains.

Once you do that and experience a little bit of success, you'll feel empowered to keep going. When you give yourself permission to fail, and to learn from that failure, you'll build a better system. It won't happen all at once.

"The more complete the system is," writes David Allen, "the more you'll trust it. And the more you trust it, the more complete you'll be motivated to keep it."

A complete system means controlling the incoming flow. Living with indoor plumbing means a lifetime of fixing leaks. And so it will be with your organizing system.

BE AGILE: HOW WE CAN VIEW ORGANIZING SYSTEMS LIKE A PIECE OF COMPUTER SOFTWARE

Long ago, I gave up learning to write computer programs. I was really interested at one point, but our household functions at peak efficiency when one of us writes prose and the other writes code.

However, if we can view organizing systems like a machine (e.g. a car), we can also liken them to computer software. This may even be more apt, given the fact that software can accept many small changes on its way to the final product. It can also fail catastrophically, only to be resurrected with an emergency update. In other words, software can adapt to its environment and the needs of its users, and it should be able to do this fairly easily.

At first, I thought a chapter about Agile Software Development — an approach to writing software that does the above with ease and grace — wouldn't feel relatable to the average person. Not everyone is a nerd married into a family of nerds, after all. Then I received an email from a decidedly non-nerdy friend with a link to a TED talk about applying Agile principles to your family.[39] As it turns out, Agile's trendiness extends beyond the realm of software development.

I'm not surprised. The Agile Manifesto was born from a need to adapt to change. Its creators rejected the idea of process for its own sake and chose to focus on individuals and relationships instead.[40] You can see how this might benefit someone with Rubin's Rebel tendency or someone with ADHD who needs an individualized solution. The message is clear: we live in a fast-paced world. We need to stay on our toes and be ready to change course at any time. These concepts are a natural fit for almost any organization or system — including your home and family.

If you're tech-averse or otherwise completely uninterested in software development, no need to worry. I'm going to spell out five of Agile's 12 core principles,[41] modified slightly to suit our goals. You'll find these principles tie nicely to every chapter of this book.

Build [systems] around motivated individuals. Give them the environment and support they need, and trust them to get the job done.

In other words, find your Why and get to know yourself. In your eagerness to get an organizational system up and running, make sure you're motivated for the long term. Know *why* you're doing this work — why it's important to *you*. Motivation must come from within.

But motivation alone won't keep you going. Set yourself up for success. Don't go overboard, but give yourself the environment and the tools you need. For tedious or focus-intensive tasks, choose a time of day when you're on top of your game. That means when your medication is at peak effectiveness, if that's part of your treatment plan, or perhaps after you finish working out. Get support from a friend if getting started feels too overwhelming. If you get distracted easily, give yourself a workstation away out of the fray. (I'm fortunate enough to have a home office with a door that closes, but the dining room table will do if you use it when the rest of the family is out of the house.) Remember *Rule #1: You Must Make Peace With Reality*. Don't fight your brain, accommodate it.

---

39 (Feiler, 2013)
40 (Highsmith, 2001)
41 (The Agile Alliance, 2001)

[A working system] is the primary measure of progress.

Let go of your visions of perfection. Let go of lofty, intimidating goals like "I'm going to have my entire office completely organized by the end of the month." Forget your visions of what an organizational system should look like, or what you should be able to do. If something is working at the most basic level, you're on the right track. Organizing your life is an iterative process. Get a basic system working and go from there.

Simplicity — the art of maximizing the amount of work not done — is essential.

Did you think you read it wrong at first? You didn't.

This could be my life motto. It's a variant of "work smarter, not harder," but it gets right to the most important point: work is hard. Do as little as possible while still maintaining a functioning system. Find ways to eliminate steps and barriers everywhere you can.

Agile processes promote sustainable [systems]. [You] should be able to maintain a constant pace indefinitely.

Have you ever started a new habit with gusto, only to abandon it a month later? You're not alone. People with ADHD have a lot of trouble sustaining effort and habits for the long term.

Part of this may stem from our zeal for starting new projects before thinking them through. Out of sight, out of mind comes back to haunt us when we try to form habits. We're poor judges of how much time and effort a new project or habit will take. We also have trouble with our *prospective memory*: we have a poor grasp on tasks we already need to complete in the future,[42] and we fail to account for how they might conflict with new additions to our plate.

What does this mean for our organizing systems? First, it means you need to abandon black-and-white thinking. Resist the temptation to go all-in on a system someone else tells you is the best. Be willing to change, to fail, to learn, and to start over again.

Also, remember *Rule #1* and accept your reality. Don't force yourself through a process because you think you should. If you have to force yourself, the system isn't sustainable. You won't continue it beyond the honeymoon period.

---

42   (Kolberg & Nadeau, 2002)

You'll need to push yourself through your initial slash-and-burn. If you've accumulated significant chaos and clutter, the cleanup will be its own project. The maintenance should not be. Be realistic as you set up your ongoing organizing systems. Imagine yourself doing this week in, week out, forever. Your system must suit you. It must feel right, and you must be able to sustain it indefinitely. If you can't, the system needs to change.

At regular intervals, [reflect] on how to become more effective, then tune and adjust [your] behavior accordingly.

What works at first may not work two years from now. At least once a year — more often, if you can manage it — take a big-picture look at your organizing process. Ask yourself what's working, and where you find yourself cutting corners or falling behind. Use this information not to make a character judgement ("I knew I wouldn't be able to keep this up."), but as critical information for you to hone your system. If something isn't working, it means you need to tweak it.

The central message of Agile is this: create a lean system that requires as little work as possible so you can adapt it easily to meet your own shifting needs. Evaluate it regularly. Remember that progress, not perfection, equals success. You should work at a level you can sustain past the initial push.

KEY TAKEAWAYS

- Buying a lot of pretty containers and organizing your mess into them will not create lasting change. You need to control the incoming flow of *stuff*.

- Be realistic about how much work you will actually do and what kind of organizing tools you will actually use. The initial push will be difficult, but ongoing maintenance shouldn't feel like a huge burden. If you have to force yourself to do it, you won't continue for the long haul.

- If your organizing system isn't working, you don't need to change, your system does. Embrace failure as an opportunity to learn and to make improvements.

- Never adopt a tool or system just because someone else told you it's great. Always consider your brain and your reality. Do what will work for you.

- Maximize the amount of work *not done*. Make sure your system requires as little work as possible.

GETTING THINGS DONE: THE HOLY GRAIL OF ORGANIZING WITH ADHD

I've read a lot of books about getting organized. *Getting Things Done* was the one that changed my life forever. Before I go any further, let's get one thing straight: I want you to read *Getting Things Done*. You don't need to put this book down and go buy it right now, but you should put it on your list. It's available as an eBook, audiobook, or paperback, depending on your reading preference. You won't regret it.

That said, many people with ADHD fail to set up and maintain a GTD system. I've participated in several private and public ADHD discussion and support groups over the years. None have quite known what to do with GTD. It sounds great, but some find it too rigid or overwhelming. Even more seem to say, "I'd love to be able to do that, but I don't know where to start."

That's why I'm here. While I hope you'll read *Getting Things Done* someday, I know (*Rule #1*, right?) you might not be there quite yet. In this section, we'll apply what we've learned so far to the core, can't-miss principles of GTD. We'll also talk about a few ADHD-specific pitfalls.

IF YOU'RE HELPING SOMEONE ELSE...

Creating a system to organize a whole life of chaos is hard work! You've probably noticed people with ADHD tend to resist tasks that feel too overwhelming, tedious, difficult, or time-consuming. The initial push to get organized may be all of the above.

Much as neither of you may want to admit it, your person with ADHD may need you to hand-hold — sometimes literally. This doesn't mean doing the work for them. However, your person will benefit from your presence alone, even if you just sit with them while they work.

Or you may want to take a more active role. For example, I once placed a big stack of books on the floor along with sheets of paper that said "keep" and "give away." I called my husband in and asked him to pick up each book in the stack and place it on top of one of the two sheets of paper. He did this easily, whereas I've never had success asking him a more open-ended, "Can you look at your books on this shelf and decide what you want to keep?" That kind of request ends one of two ways: keeping all the books or avoiding the task altogether.

I've found it's common among people with ADHD to resist or become overwhelmed by open-ended tasks. Creating a little bit of structure with those two sheets of paper made all the difference for my husband.

Think about the things you've asked of your person in the past. Are they big, nebulous things where she might not know where to start? When confronted with a big mess, many people simply freeze. Give a clear, easy starting point, along with a clear process, and you may be surprised at what she's willing (and able) to do.

REDEFINING PROJECT MANAGEMENT

Before you sit down to get your life in order, take a moment to mentally close out *Rule #2*. Have you truly contained *everything*? Remember: your brain should be used for processing, not storage. If you're still experiencing background stress and anxiety about something you haven't written down or otherwise contained, stop reading and do it now.

You've probably added a big stack of notes to the collection of physical items already in your home — everything that was in your brain which you've now made tangible. Once you've captured all this stuff, it has to go somewhere. That somewhere cannot be the surface of your desk, the couch, or — our family's personal favorite — the top of the piano. In other words, you've contained everything and created an overfilled inbox. Some items can be addressed at once. Others will require multiple steps to reach completion. For the latter, you need an easy-to-use system to keep them organized and accessible. Ideally, you should have an idea of what this system looks like before you start processing your inbox. That's what we'll do here.

You're now ready to start defining and organizing your life's projects.

FOR STARTERS: LET'S DEFINE 'PROJECT'

In *Getting Things Done*, David Allen defines a project as anything with "more than one action needed to achieve a desired result."[43] This is considerably broader than the definition I began with at the start of my organizing journey.

Project sounds so formal, doesn't it? Or sometimes like a lament: "Oh, it turned into a whole big project." But really, anything we have to keep track of through more than one task is a project. Remodeling our kitchen was a project, but so is getting our family's flu shots every October. I have to find out when the pharmacy starts offering them; assess the best time for all of us to go, based on our schedules; put it on the calendar; and make sure it happens on the assigned day. See? Project. And for someone with ADHD trying to manage a group of people with ADHD, it's even more so.

Keep this in mind as we move forward. Viewing something as simple as a flu shot as a project will encourage you to give it proper respect. When you have a system for reviewing your list of projects-in-progress, you'll prompt yourself to wonder, *where am I on getting our flu shots?*

It may also shed light on why this category of task simply isn't happening in your life. If you've written "get flu shot" on a to-do list somewhere, you're asking your brain to reinterpret that reminder every time you see it. What does "get flu shot" actually mean? What would I need to do to make that happen? Well, I don't have time to do it today, so... And another day goes by.

Don't forget the ADHD brain's working memory deficits. When your to-do list is populated by items like "get flu shot," you're asking your brain to hold all the steps to that task in mind at once. As you try to keep a grasp on all the pieces — What pharmacy should I go to? Do they have the shot available yet? When can my husband and I get there together? What about kids? I guess I have to make a doctor's appointment for my son to get it — your brain won't be able to manage it all at once. When this happens, a familiar, negative feeling sets in. The worse you feel, the less likely you are to complete that task — ever.

So give projects their due. If you need to do more than one thing to finish the job, or if the one thing you need to do can't happen yet because you're waiting on something else, it's a project. Respect it as such and put it into your project list, which is different than your to-do list. As a side benefit, creating a project list may reveal that you have too many. You may decide to delay some of your projects or not accept any more until you've finished something else. Viewing projects this way helps provide perspective on how much you *actually* have on your plate right now.

---

43 (Allen, 2015)

This may feel overwhelming at first. Stay the course. People with ADHD often lack the perspective to see the big picture unless it's spelled out in front of us. Once you do spell it out in the form of a real, complete project list, you may learn why you've felt so frazzled. But now you have a choice where you previously did not. My ADHD, before I addressed my symptoms and started getting organized, left me with a vague knowledge that I had too much to do, but I could rarely recall what any of it was. Now I can see a clear picture of my current project commitments whenever I like. And if it's too much, I can choose which projects to defer for later or drop entirely. Previously, this had all been left to chance — or even worse, my unreliable memory.

HOW TO ORGANIZE YOUR PROJECTS

Before you go pulling things out of your inbox, make sure you have a place to create and store any projects you find.

As I mentioned earlier, I use an app to do this. It's called Toodledo, and it has been around for several years. There are many apps on the market, and you can find them easily by searching online for "best GTD app" or something similar. I haven't found any free apps with Toodledo's level of support for GTD. The app was clearly written with GTD in mind, so users don't have to find clunky workarounds to use key components of the system. While Toodledo offers a paid version, most users — myself included — won't need any of the paid features to get up and running.

If an app will work for you, I recommend using one that will sync across devices. A service that offers both a web and mobile app will give you access to your projects and tasks from your phone, tablet, or computer. When you travel, your entire project management system can come with you. Adjustments are easy, and don't require you to rearrange a physical system or make changes one-by-one to a text document. An app will do a lot of the work for you and reduce barriers to using your organizing system. For people with ADHD, ease of use should be a primary consideration.

However, your situation may preclude you from using an app. Maybe you want to be able to see your project list at work but your office firewall blocks the website. Maybe you spend long periods of time without internet access. Maybe you don't own a smartphone but still need to manage your tasks and projects on the go. Or, maybe you're just more of a pen-and-paper person. Honor your unique life and brain. Don't try to force an app into your life if it doesn't feel right.

Regardless of what tool you choose, it should have the following features/capabilities:

- Can create projects or folders, inside of which you can store individual tasks and reminders.

- Easy to check off tasks when complete.

- Able to sort tasks into "contexts," or situations where you can complete them (we'll get to this in more detail later); examples include work, errands, home, computer, desk, phone, etc.

- Able to categorize tasks within a project into the following: stuff you can do right now, loose ends you're waiting on from someone else, and stuff you need to do after another task gets done (Toodledo's drop-down menu allows you to define a task as Next Action, Waiting, Delegated, etc.).

In an ideal world, you'd also want the ability to define recurring tasks, but it's not a deal-breaker. For example, the filter in my washing machine ought to be cleaned every month. When I check it off, Toodledo automatically recreates it with a due date one month from now. If I didn't have that feature, I'd just put a reminder on next month's calendar to add it to my to-do list. You also may want the option to define due dates, though I personally keep those out of my project management system. Due dates go on my calendar, not in the to-do list I check whenever I have time. This ensures I don't miss them. You might be drawn to any number of extra features, but make sure whatever you choose meets the requirements in my list above.

If you choose not to use an app, you can use paper in a binder or notebook, or you can create a spreadsheet to store this information. Use whatever feels comfortable to you, so long as it allows you to sort your tasks by project, context, and status.

Why am I asking you to think about all this now, before I've even discussed these elements of your system? Because the start-up cost of setting up a project management system is high. If you spend hours entering your tasks and projects into a document or app, only to find it lacks a necessary feature, you may feel too discouraged to start over. If you try to make an ineffective tool work for you just because you can't imagine doing the tedious initial data entry all over again, your brain will resist using it. Staying organized will feel like a negative experience and your whole effort to get control of your life may fail. Before you commit to a tool by putting your information (and time) into it, make sure it will do what you need it to do. Make sure it feels right and you look forward to using it every day.

KEY TAKEAWAYS

- If you're not ready to tackle the full GTD system yet, you can get started with a few core principles outlined in this book.

- A project is anything that requires more than a single task to get it done. For example: getting your family's flu vaccinations.

- When you begin defining projects properly, you may realize you have too much on your plate.

- Choose a project management system (app, spreadsheet, paper-based, etc.) based on your needs and preferences. Make sure it feels comfortable to you.

EMPTY THAT INBOX

Okay. You have a project management system, a filing cabinet (or rack, or box) with hanging folders, a labelmaker if you're feeling fancy, and some containers. Maybe you even took my advice and bought one of those little document scanners or downloaded a smartphone app to serve the purpose. Good for you.

Now we're ready to empty that inbox. Lots of people with ADHD believe they can't reach David Allen's exalted Inbox Zero. I'm here to tell you it can be done. It does, however, require some discipline that won't always come easily.

Your inbox probably has a mix of the following: immediately actionable items, contributions to a new or existing project, and stuff that just needs to be filed or put away. Hopefully it contains everything that's been making you feel overwhelmed.

Now let's take a look at how to deal with it all. Bookmark the graphic on the next page (Figure 4). If you get lost, refer back to it for a big-picture idea of what we want to accomplish as we set up our system:

1. **Pick a system**. We discussed this in the previous chapter about project management; I use Toodledo to track my projects.

2. **Grab your inbox(es)**.

3. Take stuff out **one piece at a time**.

4. **Assess whether it's a two-to-five-minute task**, like a piece of filing or a receipt from the grocery store, or something bigger. The short tasks should be done immediately, whereas the bigger ones will go into your project/task management system.

From this humble process, great progress is made. Let's get started!

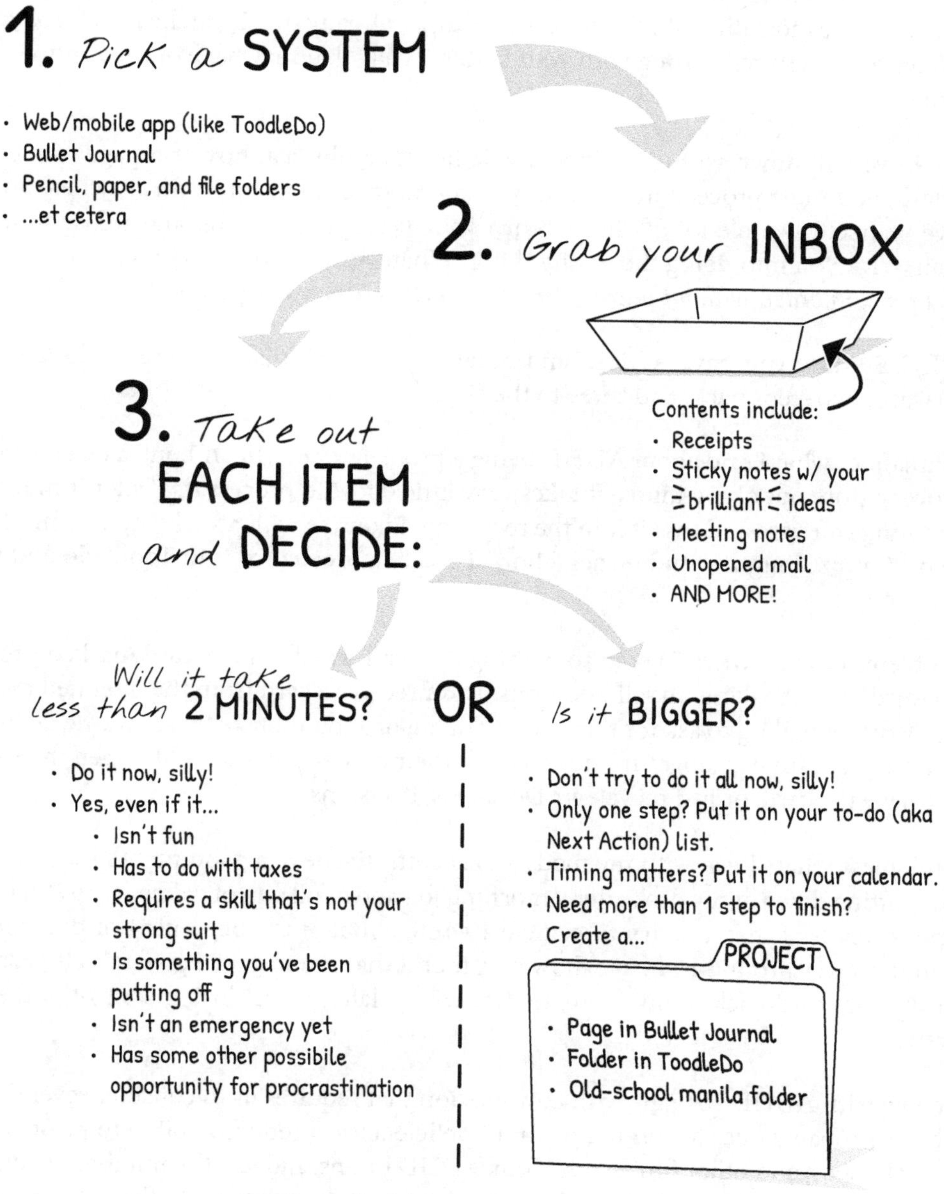

1. *Pick a* **SYSTEM**

- Web/mobile app (like ToodleDo)
- Bullet Journal
- Pencil, paper, and file folders
- ...et cetera

2. *Grab your* **INBOX**

Contents include:
- Receipts
- Sticky notes w/ your ≡brilliant≡ ideas
- Meeting notes
- Unopened mail
- AND MORE!

3. *Take out* **EACH ITEM** *and* **DECIDE:**

Will it take *less than* **2 MINUTES?** **OR** *Is it* **BIGGER?**

- Do it now, silly!
- Yes, even if it...
  - Isn't fun
  - Has to do with taxes
  - Requires a skill that's not your strong suit
  - Is something you've been putting off
  - Isn't an emergency yet
  - Has some other possible opportunity for procrastination

- Don't try to do it all now, silly!
- Only one step? Put it on your to-do (aka Next Action) list.
- Timing matters? Put it on your calendar.
- Need more than 1 step to finish? Create a...

PROJECT
- Page in Bullet Journal
- Folder in ToodleDo
- Old-school manila folder

Figure 4 Inbox Flow

ONE THING AT A TIME, IN FORWARD, NOT REVERSE

In all the organizing I do for my business, writing, and family, there's one thing I find far and away the most difficult. I've told you 53 times already that if you have to force yourself too hard, something's wrong with your system. Well, you may have one exception. This is mine.

When you sit down with your inbox, whether it's a physical box or a page of unopened emails, you must proceed in an orderly fashion. Rebels, I'm sorry, this is where you can't give yourself a whole lot of choice. Turn your perception around and refuse to let your brain trick you into doing the wrong thing. Whatever you do, empty your inbox *one item at a time, in order, without putting anything back in once you take it out.*

Why? Because you have ADHD, and because you won't make progress taking one step forward, two steps back, and three to the side.

Remember what I said about ADHD being a problem of inertia. If I pull a receipt from the grocery store out of my inbox, it takes very little effort to process it. I enter it into our accounting software and toss it into the recycling. Likewise with a sticky note reminding me to plan a pizza night with our neighbors. I create a project for it in Toodledo and recycle the note.

Problems crop up when I get to something like a returned holiday card marked "unable to forward." I start asking myself questions. Did I receive a card from the intended recipient? Is it worth emailing to ask for their new address, or should I take this as the de facto end of our holiday card exchange? If I don't ask for their new address, should I open the envelope and save the card, or just recycle it? Decisions, decisions.

And guess what? Even with my meds at peak effectiveness, a good night's sleep under my belt, sitting down at my desk after a morning jog and a full cup of coffee, I can still encounter a version of that laundry force field I wrote about at the beginning of this book. I've found no way around it. I have, however, found that the instant I give myself permission to slip that card back in my inbox to deal with it later, I start losing control of the whole system.

People with ADHD struggle with any decision that requires us to consider several factors. This is probably due to working memory deficiencies, a reduced ability to prioritize individual issues, and other fun facets of our ADHD brains. Indeed, the number of confounding issues with that returned holiday card alone could turn me off to the entire inbox.

Unfortunately, there's no easy way around this. All I can tell you is you have to get comfortable with being uncomfortable. Practice pushing yourself through that initial resistance. You might not always succeed, and that's okay. Identifying the issue and practicing overcoming it will help you a lot in the long term. At the very least, these small victories will teach you that success is *possible*, and this force field isn't impenetrable.

I find it helpful to talk to myself through more challenging decisions, or to write a list of considerations. For example: okay, this card was returned in the mail. Have I communicated with this person at all this year? Would I feel awkward reaching out for their address, given how little we've spoken? Alright, well, let's think about getting back in touch but not send them a card, how's that? How many extra cards do I have? Okay, let's bite the bullet and just dump the whole thing in the recycling without opening it.

Don't forget *Rule #1*: accept that this — a world where deciding what to do with a piece of returned mail becomes a whole process — is your reality. Be compassionate and objective. Don't judge or put yourself down. Accept and respect the fact that some of the little things in your inbox are really hard for you to deal with, and that's part of why you've found it so hard to get organized.

And know, without a doubt, that you have to practice this important new skill: once you pull something from your inbox, it doesn't go back in.

IF YOU'RE HELPING SOMEONE ELSE...

It's easy to get annoyed by the little things, like a single piece of returned mail, that seem to clog up the whole system. Why can't your person with ADHD just deal with it already?

I hope this section has helped you to understand there is no "just dealing" with some things. Sorry to disappoint, but it's just the way it is. This will remain true to some extent even with an ideal treatment plan in place.

You have two options if you want to help move things along: one, you can keep an eye out for these one-off issues and deal with them yourself. (You can even be sassy about it and say, "For heaven's sake, just put it in the recycling!" while flinging it into the bin.) Or you can help talk your person through the decision-making process. Help identify the snag and ask specific questions to guide them to the most sensible course of action.

It's a classic case of giving the person with ADHD a fish or teaching him to fish for himself. If you teach him to fish at every opportunity, you'll both end up exhausted. In the beginning, at least, expect to do more things for her than you might find ideal in the long term. As she gains confidence, she'll be more receptive to tackling things that overwhelmed her in the past.

YOU CAN'T DO IT ALL NOW

The second-biggest challenge to reaching Inbox Zero with ADHD is resisting the temptation to do everything, completely, as it comes up.

Maybe you're afraid you'll forget to take care of it unless you do it now. This is understandable, given your past. But we're setting up a new system here, and you must learn to trust it. This is like the symptom management feedback loop: the more you trust the system, the more you'll use and maintain it. The more you use and maintain it, the more you'll be able to trust it. If you allow yourself to step outside your system, you'll lose motivation to keep it running smoothly.

When pulling items (one at a time) out of my inbox, I resolve some of them right away. Receipts, for example, or bills that require me to write a check. That's because these tasks will take between two and five minutes and aren't worth putting into my to-do list.

However, a person with ADHD can easily be derailed by the item we pull out and exclaim, "Oooh! I forgot about this! Let me take care of it right now…" An hour goes by and we still have a full inbox. Even if we aren't victims of the forgetting fear mentioned above, we can get roped into something that sounds more fun, like planning a ski vacation, rather than deciding what to do with that returned holiday card.

If you have ADHD, you know you can always, *always* find something more appealing than that thing you don't want to do. The temptation to work on a fun item from your inbox at the expense of everything else in there is strong. Resist it. If the task will take you more than a couple minutes, put it into your project management system and move on.

Of course, you will succumb to temptation. When you do, look at that inbox. Remember that it's still full because you got sidetracked! Next time, consider setting a timer for a task so you don't get sucked in. I particularly love sand timers (we have a few two-minute sand timers in our house, in addition to a five- and ten-minute timer) because they physically represent the passage of time. The Time Timer does this in the form of a disappearing red wedge on a clock face and allows you to set it to any amount of time you like.

Bottom line: your inbox feeds your project management system and your filing system. If you can manage a continuation of the plumbing analogy, think of it this way: the pipe delivering water to your house is supposed to feed everything in your house that requires water. You don't need to use it all right when it comes in. You just need a system in place to make sure it gets to your sink, toilet, dishwasher, and shower — and doesn't flood your basement.

So quit drinking from the pipe. You can knock out very short tasks while emptying your inbox, but avoid stopping for anything over two minutes. Otherwise, your inbox will never be empty. I know it's hard to do when you have ADHD, but you need to try your best every time.

KEY TAKEAWAYS

- Empty your inbox one thing at a time, in order.

- Resist the temptation to skip around and work on more fun or interesting projects first.

- If you can do a task in two to five minutes, go ahead and do it; if not, put it into your task/project management system and move on.

- Never put something back into your inbox once you take it out.

- Some items in the inbox that look simple (e.g. a returned holiday card) can overwhelm a person with ADHD.

HOW TO FILE

As you go through your inbox, some things will end up in the trash, recycling, or shredder. Others will be put away in their proper home. And yet others will need a home.

A general rule: if it can fit in a hanging file, store it there. Hanging files give you an excellent place to corral, organize, and label your stuff. Don't shortchange yourself by limiting their usefulness to paper.

People with ADHD tend to latch onto ideas. We often see and generate fewer solutions to problems than neurotypical folks do.[44] In my personal experience, this leads to solutions that seem brilliant at the time, but hare-brained in hindsight. A tiny item will be stored in the most ingenious place thanks to a connection my brain grabbed onto and wouldn't let go. Later, I'll spend hours trying to reverse-engineer my thought process. I may never find the item again.

I solved this problem in our household by shamelessly filing everything I can, and doing it alphabetically.

---

44 (Barkley, 2010)

Everyone Knows the Alphabet

As a writer, I often think in terms of narratives. Perhaps this explains my love for categorizing my files and possessions. I used to label hanging files by category, then stuff them full of file folders. I created bins for various A/V equipment and computer accessories and stored them in the basement. Even a messy stack of junk on the floor had some kind of story.

Lots of people try to organize this way. The problem is, what seems an obvious connection to you may be surprisingly opaque to another person. If you have ADHD, and especially if you have a poor memory, your month-ago self can sometimes *feel* like another person.

Don't put yourself in a position where you or anyone else are forced to retrace your steps. Your filing cabinet should be organized alphabetically — period. Each hanging file should contain one, and only one, folder. That folder should be labeled clearly and, if not printed from a label maker, written in neat, dark print. Nobody should need to put themselves inside your brain to figure out where to find an important document.

While you're at it, remove the guesswork from locating the spare gasket for your garden hose, the buttons that came with your suit jacket, and the paint chips you grabbed from the hardware store last week. These items are all small enough for a file folder. My flatbed scanner has a removable plastic tray for scanning negatives. I store this in a hanging file in my file cabinet. I would have no hope of finding it when I need it otherwise.

Let's face it: your home won't always be the picture of tidiness. Those tiny items are the first to get lost in the shuffle. Rather than overturning your junk drawer in a panic when you need that spare button, file it, even if you feel silly doing so. It'll help you out when other parts of your home make it tough to find the little stuff.

Make Your Files Comfortable

In *The Life-Changing Magic of Tidying Up*, organizing guru Marie Kondo talks a lot about making your possessions comfortable. She advises against cramming your dresser drawers too full or stressing your socks by balling rather than folding them.[45]

You'll have to ask your socks for their storage preference, but your file folders definitely need to breathe. Beware the ADHD force field, which will never fully dissipate from your filing responsibilities. A file cabinet that's messy and so crammed that you can't easily add or remove anything from it will lead back to the problem that brought you there in the first place: piles.

---

45   (Kondo, 2014)

Avoid anything that gives you any reason at all to place even one item in a "to be filed" pile. This includes overstuffed drawers, silly-colored folders (or non-silly-colored folders, depending on your preference), poor labeling, an obscure (i.e. non-alphabetical) filing system, a labelmaker that keeps disappearing from your desk, etc. If you prefer an open filing rack to a traditional filing cabinet with drawers, go for it. The bottom line is, if you're going to bother keeping these files, they should be useful for you. If you're not maintaining them in a system that works for you and your household, they're not useful.

SCAN AND SHRED

In his book *The Nerdist Way*, entertainer Chris Hardwick swears by what he calls "the two Ss: SCAN and SHRED."[46] Unless you possess a deep love for filing, and for pruning those files at least once annually, take this advice to heart.

There are some documents I will not shred; mortgage and tax documents come to mind. If it can possibly be shredded (or recycled), it never makes it into my filing cabinet. This includes bills, bank statements, medical documents, and the like.

Adopting a scan-and-shred policy whenever possible will benefit you in a few ways. First, you won't need to go through the process I described earlier: get out a file folder and a hanging file, print (or write) a label on it, and fit it into your alphabetical filing system. The definition of tedium, right? And then you need to remember to go through that filing cabinet once a year to remove everything you no longer need. I don't think so. No one with ADHD needs this.

The second benefit is a biggie. Despite your strict adherence to your alphabetical system, you will mess up sometimes. Or you or your family will file something differently than the seeker would have, thereby rendering the alphabetical system useless. My husband recently spent a long time searching for our car's inspection documents, which I'd filed under E for emissions inspection. He looked under H for Honda and A for auto, only finding the folder when he looked at each folder in the cabinet individually. We had a similar issue when I filed his Technic LEGOs instructions under T.

Here's the great thing about scan and shred: if you title your document well, you cannot lose it. It doesn't matter whether you put the emissions inspection ticket in a folder titled Emissions, Honda, or Auto. While you're doing other things, your computer is busy scanning all those filenames and indexing them for future reference. When you type "inspection" into the search bar at the top of your file window, it'll find it in less than a second.

---

46 (Hardwick, 2014)

Of course, I still highly recommend a simple system of file folders, even on the computer. I'm a tactile person, remember? We appreciate being able to click through a sequence of folders to find what we need. I almost never use my computer's search function unless I really can't find something. Chances are, if you live or work with another person, someone else will need to navigate your electronic files at some point. Or you'll forget what you titled a document. For those times, you'll be thankful you created a folder for those LEGO manuals.

A last word: when you institute a scan-and-shred policy, you should already have a reliable backup system in place. It's so easy to do, there's really no excuse for losing a file to hardware failure, a bad computer virus, or accidental deletion. I store most of my files in Dropbox or Google Drive, and I use a cloud backup service on my desktop computer. Dropbox and Google Drive sync to other devices — like a laptop or mobile device — so your files aren't just in the cloud, they're on multiple hard drives that you personally own. A dedicated backup service like Carbonite or Backblaze adds an extra layer of protection.

KEY TAKEAWAYS

- Scan and shred (or recycle) whatever you can to reduce filing clutter.
- File alphabetically, not by category.
- Use hanging files, and keep only one folder in each.
- Label folders clearly in neat, dark ink or with a labelmaker.
- Use an automated backup service to protect your digital files.
- Make your files easy for others to read and navigate.

POPULATE YOUR TO-DO LIST WITH STUFF YOU CAN ACTUALLY DO

As you empty your inbox, you'll find yourself with lots of items that need to be added to your to-do list. That's great, if that to-do list is full of things you can actually *do*.

Keep in mind the GTD definition of a project: anything that requires more than a single, discrete action. Combine this with the knowledge that ADHD cripples our working memory, or the ability to hold more than one thing in mind at once. This means when you fill a to-do list with tasks that are actually *projects*, you have a recipe for overwhelm. You're asking your brain to look at a complex (i.e. more than single-step) task, break it down, and identify the next step. It's like trying to solve a calculus problem without a pencil and paper. Some people can do this in their heads, but this book isn't about them.

"Many projects seem overwhelming," Allen writes in *Getting Things Done*, "and they *are* overwhelming because you can't *do* a project at all! You can only do an action related to it." It's this related action that should go on your to-do list, and nothing else (for an example, see Figure 6). Otherwise, you will continue to view your to-do list as a big pile of stuff that probably won't get done.

For example, I have a big painting I want to hang above my bed. It's tempting to write, "hang big painting above bed" on a to-do list. And that would be one way to guarantee it will never get done because there are several steps required to achieve the result. We have brick walls, which require a hammer drill to install an anchor big enough to hang anything heavy. The painting itself doesn't have any hanging hardware on the back. Hanging the picture is therefore a *project*, not a task.

Instead of a to-do item to hang the picture, I need to create a project for it in my project management app (i.e. Toodledo). Then I need to create a to-do item for "look for picture hanging supplies in basement." This is the very next action I could take on the project, and it's quite easy to do — as long as I'm at home, which leads me to my next point.

In addition to being possible at all, items on your to-do list should be possible *in your current context*. The concept of context was one of the greatest gifts given to me by GTD. Do you think someone who struggles to read instructions, complete a list in order, or pay attention long enough to complete a single task can weed irrelevant items out of a to-do list? I know I can't, and I don't.

Instead, I organize my to-do list — full of simple, single tasks that are truly the very next action I need to take — by context. In GTD terms, a task's context is defined by the tool, location, or situation needed to complete it.[47] Some contexts may depend on other people, while some will be determined by where you are, either physically or mentally. As of this writing, my contexts are as follows (you can see a real-life example in Figure 5):

- *House (anytime)*, *House (while my son's asleep)*, and *House (while my son's awake)*, for tasks that require my kid to be awake or asleep (or can be done anytime).
- *Outdoors*, which I pull out while watching my son ride his bike, or on days when I'm desperate for fresh air myself.
- *Weekend*, for when I need a lot of uninterrupted time, and/or I can't include my son in the project.
- *Basement/Craft Room.*

---

47 (Allen, 2015)

- *Computer (any)*, *Computer (desktop PC)*, and *Computer (MacBook)*, because I have different software on each device.

- *Phone (talking)* and *Phone (texting)*.

- *Desk*, for tasks that require me to sit at my desk but not use a computer.

- *Errands*.

- *Television*, for tasks I can do in front of the TV.

I also maintain contexts for people I often need to talk to, like my husband and my mom. When they're with me, I sneak a look at my context for them and try to act as natural as possible as I make my way through the list.

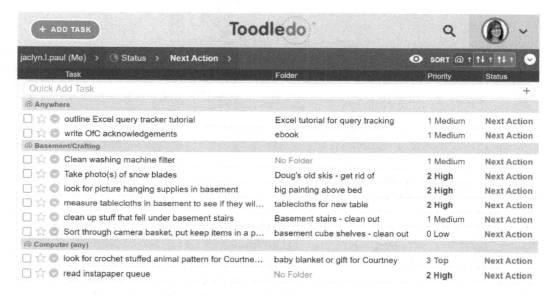

Figure 5 An excerpt from my to-do list in Toodledo

Your life and its constraints will determine how many or how few contexts you have. Your goal is to reduce the amount you're asking of your brain. It's already doing you a favor by looking at the to-do list in the first place and considering completing an item from it. Don't shove a jumble in its face that it must untangle to figure out what might be actionable.

Once you get to the point where you're pulling out a to-do list, you need to make sure it's a list of stuff you can *actually do in the moment*. This will allow you to take advantage of any available sliver of productive time, no matter where you are or who you're with. It will also help you capitalize on your ADHD inertia. Once I'm on the phone, my brain is in phone mode. Even though I hate talking on the phone, I will make four more phone calls just because it's easier than switching to a different kind of task.

KEY TAKEAWAYS

- Fill your to-do list only with single actions you can do with little to no preparation.

- Organize your to-do list by *context*, i.e. the tools, people, and/or location needed to complete the task.

- If you fill your to-do list with multi-step projects, you'll continue to view that to-do list as a big pile of stuff that'll never get done.

Look here (your context headings) first!

next actions

AKA your to-do list!

basement/craft room
- clean washing machine filter
- see if I have any fabric for tablecloths

computer (any)
- send email about ladies' game night
- make a list of 5k races I could register for

computer (office)
- scan stack of academic records
- print emergency kit checklist from ready.gov

husband
- discuss how to hang tall painting
- decide how many days we should spend at the beach over 4th of July

errands
- ATM
- buy beer for ski trip

house (anytime)
- re-hang office light pull chain
- check exp. dates on CO/smoke detectors

outdoors
- put new sticker on car
- clean paddleboard

phone (talking)
- schedule oil change

phone (texting)
- set up craigslist alert for dining chairs
- ask Dad for dates he can come visit

television
- mend gray and yellow socks

CONTEXT is Key: Where do I need to be? Who do I need to see? What tools do I need to get this done?

These help me use time I would otherwise waste (e.g. in a waiting room, bored).

Credit where it's due:
The concepts of Next Actions and Contexts in your to-do list come from David Allen's *Getting Things Done*.

Figure 6 *Next Actions*

TYING IT ALL TOGETHER: GET TO INBOX ZERO WITHOUT MAKING A BIG MESS

Bottom line: your inbox should be part of a system you can sustain indefinitely. That means emptying your inbox should *not* be a daunting task you feel like you have to set aside an entire day to do. The following strategies will help:

- **Empty your inbox *often*,** so it doesn't grow too huge and intimidating, and possibly require you to register it for its own zip code. I shoot for every 2-3 days for a totally empty physical inbox, less than that for email. Any longer, and I start feeling out of control and like I need to make the inbox its own project. In other words, the force field goes up.

- **Resist the urge to do all the things at once**. Let your pipeline feed the whole system as opposed to trying to resolve everything immediately as it comes in. It's hard with ADHD because we have trouble remembering the rest of the world exists. We see one important thing in our inbox and we hyperfocus on getting it done at the expense of everything else. Don't do this unless the task will take you less than five minutes — two, if you can manage it.

- **Make it easy to file stuff that needs to be filed,** so you'll file it right away. No person with ADHD is going to get jazzed about a big stack of to-be-filed papers sitting on a table.

- Remember, **if you need to do more than one simple, discrete, single-step task to finish it, it's a project**. Put it in your project management app or system and suss out the very next thing you can do to inch the process forward. Write *that* on your to-do list.

- In addition to organizing your to-do list by project, **use GTD contexts**. Think about the conditions under which you can do that task. Make sure you can bring up a list at any given moment of all the tasks you can complete right here, right now.

- Above all, **make it easy on your brain**. If your brain is willing to look at a to-do list and accomplish something on that list, don't squander this opportunity! Make sure your list is useful and includes only single actions you can actually do right now.

Doubting yourself? Thinking you'll surely end up with an overflowing inbox before too long? Take heart. Those fears are well-founded, but progress, not perfection, should be your measure of success. Even if you only keep your inbox under control for a week or two, you've given yourself a taste. You've experienced what it's like to get the car moving forward without stalling. From there, you can begin to troubleshoot. You can also say hello to loss aversion: the desire to keep what we have. Its power over human behavior is nearly unmatched. Once you know what having a clean inbox for a week feels like, you won't want to lose it.

On a daily basis, your inbox's worst enemy is overwhelm. If your ADHD brain takes one look at it and says "no way!" you're not going to get through it. You can try reducing the amount of stuff coming in (as discussed earlier, and also in future chapters) and you can empty your inbox more frequently. You can make sure your system is streamlined and easy to use. Still, you might struggle, especially at first.

Don't be afraid to ask for help. If you live with another person, try asking them to sit with you while you do your inbox. Talk out loud when you pick up an item that gives you trouble. Ask your partner to make sure you stick with the job until it's done. Over time, as you work on your organizing skills and your ADHD treatment strategy, these habits will become more deeply ingrained. For now, try not to be shy about leaning on someone else for support.

MY FRIEND THE BULLET JOURNAL

By this point, some of you may need a breather. GTD can feel overwhelming, and some people find apps like Toodledo off-putting. The next tool I'm going to tell you about doesn't work as a standalone for me, but you may feel differently. It can be both messy and flexible while still getting the job done. If you find most organizing tools stodgy or unappealing, you may benefit from a more unique and creative approach. For that, there's Bullet Journaling.

I've carried a notebook everywhere since age 12, when I first watched the movie *Harriet the Spy*. Harriet's character spoke to me: she wore baggy jeans, she was a bit of an outcast, she felt compelled to record much of her life in writing, and this writing caused her trouble and humiliation at least once. As much as Harriet felt like a version of me, I also wanted to be like her. I wanted a notebook by my side.

I started with the traditional Mead marble composition books, just like Harriet carried in the movie. I now use trendy Moleskines. Over the years, I've tried many different notebooks, always wanting the perfect one that felt *right* for that moment.

In addition to my trusty notebook, I've tried adding a day planner to my life. Each fall, my high school issued planners for us to keep track of our assignments. My college bookstores offered them for sale as well. After college, I tried a few different planner systems and eventually adopted a smartphone when those came along. Through all this, I still maintained my notebook.

The Bullet Journal system provides a set of guidelines for structuring your own notebook into a day planner, diary, notepad, and to-do list — all in one package, complete with an index. In short, it integrates a day planner with the notebook I've kept for most of my life. Like GTD, it's a system, not a product, so it can be modified to suit the individual. Bullet Journaling may provide a welcoming platform for adults with ADHD who find GTD unapproachable. A gateway drug, if you will.

You already know I use apps to stay organized with GTD, and I'm a strong advocate for apps that sync to multiple devices. So, wouldn't a notebook duplicate my work?

Kind of, but I appreciate a tactile element to my daily organization. Screens can feel too abstract. I use my notebook for everything: Grocery lists. Jotting down ideas, drafts, or outlines for writing projects. Taking notes at meetings. On-the-fly to-do lists. Goal-setting exercises. Everything imaginable.

The Bullet Journal system helps me organize those elements and keeps me from losing track of what I write down. Because I have ADHD and a very poor memory, I write nearly everything down, and I need a way to find it later.

WHAT IS A BULLET JOURNAL?

Digital product designer Ryder Carroll developed Bullet Journaling over several years of trial and error.[48] You can watch his video overview at www.bulletjournal.com. While it's meant to be a flexible system that evolves with your needs, most Bullet Journals contain these key elements:

- An *index* of all content, with page numbers.
- A *Daily Log*, to track daily schedules and to-dos week by week.
- A *Monthly Log*, to show the upcoming month at a glance.
- A *Future Log*, to outline significant goals and events for the next six months.

---

48 (Carroll, 2017)

From there, you can include a lot of other content: lists, notes, sketches, whatever you want. Here are a few sample pages from my own Bullet Journal (Figures 7-9):

daily log: november 2017

// this week:

- x mail stickers
- • finish vignettes
- x enter WD short story contest
- • write enews
- • send Coop photos
- • brainstorm final book titles
- • test smoke alarms
- • clean washing machine filter

- • Read to Reef
- • get in touch w/ Nathalie

MON
11 13

- x weekly review
- ✓ R-dentist appt
- x Contact Ms. Amy
- x pick out show & tell w/ R (H)
- x print sticker address labels

OFC WC: YOGA?

| +1921 | Y ☒ | N ☐ |

instrument:
PIANO

Cleaned up:
distributed bout
stations

TUE
11 14

- x library books due
- x PO-buy stamps, get hold mail forms
- ✓ R's swim class
- x take out trash
- ✓ MCA membership mtg
- ✓ show & tell day

OFC WC: YOGA?

| +1053 | Y ☒ | N ☐ |

instrument:
PIANO

cleaned up:
lingering kitchen
clutter

WED
11 15

- x WD short story contest deadline
- ❋ 11 lineWed
- ✓ run w/ Lisa
- x pick up Rx
- x call for R's flu shot

OFC WC: YOGA?

| +1630 | Y ☒ | N ☐ |

instrument:

cleaned up:
cleaned under
kitchen sink

(121)

Figure 7 Bullet Journal Sample Page

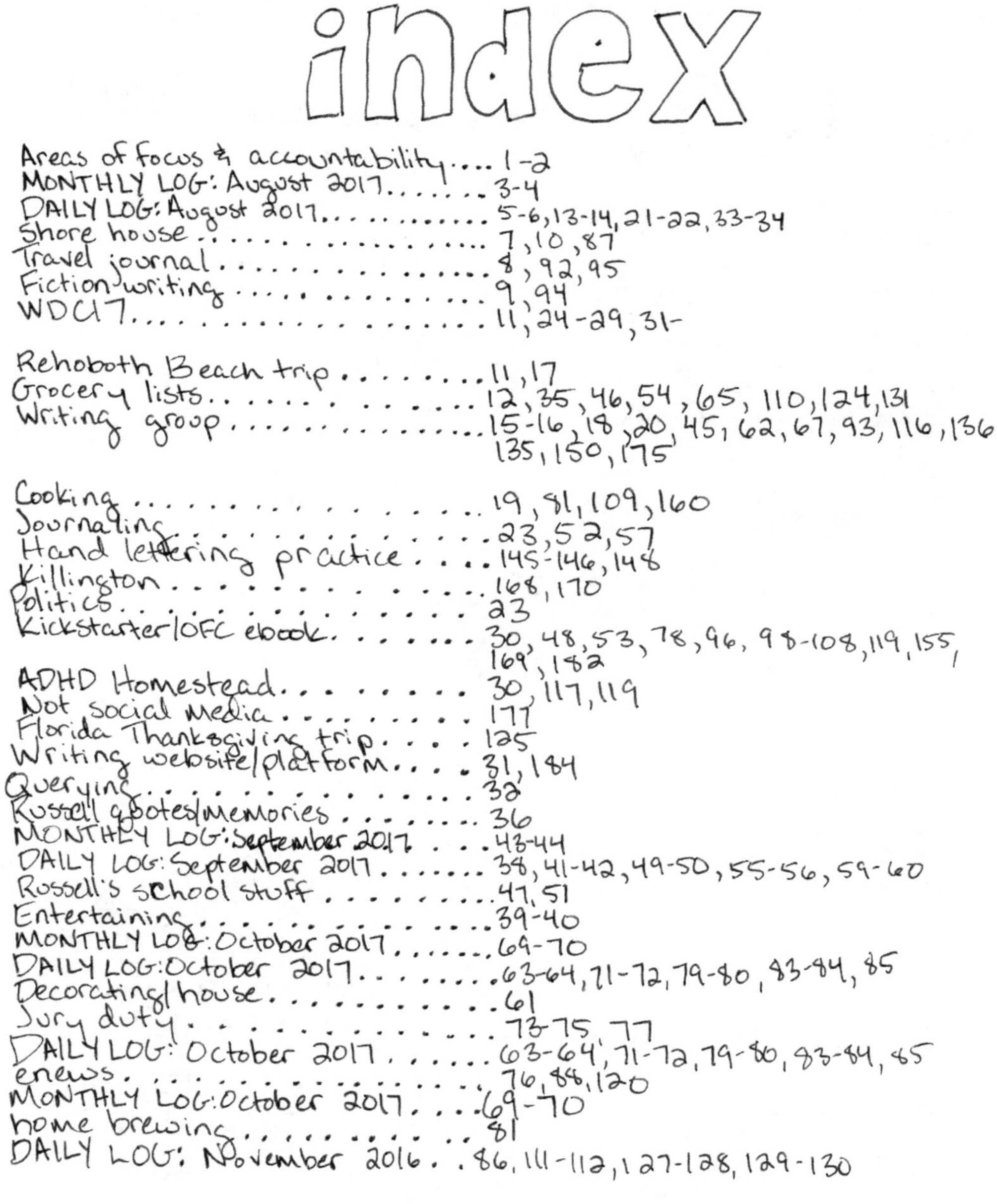

index

Figure 8 Bullet Journal Sample Page

VEGAN CHILI

INGREDIENTS

poblano pepper
carrots (2 large)
celery (2 stalks)
onion (1g yellow)
garlic (4-5 cloves)
green bell pepper
zucchini
beyond meat (crumbles)

canned green chiles x2

pinto beans (2 cans)
black beans (1 can)
kidney beans (1 can)
diced tomatoes (fire roasted, 1 28oz +
                 1 15 oz can)
salsa (med., ~1/2 cup)

chili powder (~2 palmfuls)
cumin (palmful)
oregano (palmful)

salt (while sauteeing, to taste
       after that)

smoked paprika (palmful)
garlic powder (palmful → maybe less?)

1. Saute onions, garlic, celery, carrot until soft, 5-10 min.
   Salt while cooking
2. Add peppers & zukes, & salt, cook until just begin to
   soften, ~7 min
3. Add Beyond Meat, cook 3 min or until crumbles
   are broken up & integrated
4. Add to crock b/ canned ingredients, spices; stir
   well
5. Cook on low ~4 hours

Figure 9 Bullet Journal Sample Page

My sample index gives you an idea of how many topics a Bullet Journal can cover. I use my Bullet Journal to practice hand lettering, outline blog posts, plan vacations, write grocery lists, and take notes in the kitchen.

If you want to give Bullet Journaling a try, here's what you do:

1. Watch the intro video to get a feel for the process.

2. Buy a blank notebook you will use and love.

3. Create an index.

4. Start adding your content. Add each new type of content to the index *first*, before you put the first word or sketch to paper.

CREATING A SYSTEM THAT FEELS RIGHT

If a system or a tool doesn't feel right, you won't use it. David Allen, for example, recommends a physical accordion-style tickler file in *Getting Things Done*. I just don't click with it. I've purchased these tickler files but never used them successfully. What works great for some people doesn't work great for me, and that's okay.

Adults with ADHD should remain attentive to what they like. What feels comfortable? What meshes with tools you already enjoy using? I love Bullet Journaling's infinite flexibility. I choose the size, feel, and contents of my notebook to make it something that works for me.

I currently keep my Bullet Journal in Moleskine's extra-large dotted notebook. In the spirit of Marie Kondo's KonMari method,[49] I personalize each notebook to make it feel special and joyful to have and use. I use postcards or stickers to embellish the cover and make each notebook unique.

Also, unlike store-bought planners, Bullet Journals begin as a blank slate. The introductory video suggests certain symbols and categories of content, but you're free to leave out anything that doesn't work. For example, Carroll suggests a Future Log, which examines plans and goals for the next six months. Despite my best intentions, I never ended up filling this out. I now omit it from my Bullet Journal. Neglected sections of a planner, especially those that discuss our aspirations for the future, can be a significant source of guilt. I love being

---

49   (Kondo, 2014)

able to remove that guilt by removing the unhelpful section. I still plan for the future, but I do so with a tool that works for me.

For people who dislike being told what to do or who struggle to fit their unique process and tastes into an existing system, a Bullet Journal can offer a way out. It gives you a tool to get organized without telling you how to structure it. That part you get to do on your own.

YES, I DO DUPLICATE WORK

I know, right? I keep telling you to keep it simple, maximize the amount of work *not* done, and now I'm going to confess: not only do I duplicate organizing work in my Bullet Journal, I do it by *writing longhand*. Like I said, this may not be for everyone. You may choose to use only a Bullet Journal or only an app, but some of us need a small dose of redundancy for certain things to sink in.

And what are those things? They're my obligations for this week. Each week, I copy all my appointments, reminders, and time-sensitive tasks from Google Calendar to my Daily Log. These pieces of information — the places I need to be and things I need to do over the next several days — are some of the most important in my life. They're the tidbits that will make or break my relationships with others and myself. I need this stuff in the front of my mind, always. Copying it into my Bullet Journal accomplishes this in a few ways.

First, I'm a tactile, word-oriented person. I've always preferred longhand note-taking whenever possible. Handwritten notes help me remember and understand in a way electronic records don't. There may be research to back this up: one study found that even when students focused exclusively on taking notes, not doing other things like checking Facebook or writing a paper for another class, those who typed their notes didn't internalize concepts as well as longhand note-takers. This may be because typing — especially for speedy typists like me — allows us to transcribe more of what we hear, rather than writing it in our own words.[50] Electronic notes also remove opportunities to make notes or doodles in the margins, and while they speed up the actual translation from brain to page, they don't improve the *quality* of what we write down.[51]

In my everyday life, I need to slow down this translation phase: the part where I write something down. Making it something I can hold in my hand helps the tactile part of my brain. I also suspect that the extra time it takes to handwrite a note gives my working memory a chance to grab onto it before it slips away.

---

50 (Mueller & Oppenheimer, 2014)
51 (Kellogg, 1989)

Whatever the underlying causes, I've found that handwriting my agenda at the start of each week significantly increases my awareness of what I need to do and when. Without taking that extra step, I feel adrift. Appointments and deadlines creep up on me. I forget a lot more things, and I forget more often. It's worth the extra 10 minutes I spend every week to take some old-fashioned, handwritten notes about my upcoming commitments.

But there's another reason I copy my Daily Log longhand into my Bullet Journal: it untethers me from my computer and smart phone. I can put my schedule, reminders, and deadlines in front of my face first thing in the morning without starting my day staring at a screen. I can organize my life anywhere, even off the grid or in situations where putting myself behind a screen would feel inappropriate or antisocial. And that's exactly what I do.

To show you what I mean, let me walk you through my Bullet Journal's daily grind.

A DAY IN THE LIFE OF MY BULLET JOURNAL

While very few pages of my present-day notebook offer content worthy of *Harriet the Spy*, I still carry it everywhere. In fact, my notebook spends more time by my side than my smart phone. Think back to *Rule #2: You Need a Container*. I keep my smartphone as contained as possible. While I rely on it when I'm on the go, I don't want it to be my primary source of notifications and reminders when I'm working or relaxing at home. My Bullet Journal fills the gap. It gives me an offline summary of the most important information, the things I need to know and do today. It allows me to feel comfortable putting my phone out of reach for hours at a time.

Here's what an average day with my Bullet Journal looks like:

Morning

I wake up and walk downstairs. My Bullet Journal covers my place at the breakfast table, open to this week's Daily Log. I look to see what's going on today and what I need to get done. If any of that involves others in my household, now is the time to discuss it, before everyone leaves for school and work. I also make sure everything I need to send to school with my kiddo is in his bag.

At some point, I may check my phone, but I don't do it first thing. That's what the Bullet Journal is for.

Work/School Day

Once everyone leaves, the house quiets down, and my meds kick in, I head to my office with my Bullet Journal. After a quick scan of my email, I start working on the day's tasks and prepare for any meetings I have that day.

Only after today's must-do tasks from the Bullet Journal are complete do I look at my to-do list of Next Actions in Toodledo. My phone usually stays downstairs in the cell phone bin.

If I leave the house/office for any errands or meetings, my Bullet Journal comes with me. I use it to take notes, to do reflection and planning while I wait for meetings to begin, and as a list if I'm going to the store. My phone comes with me, too, but I try to leave it in my bag if I'm with other people. I will use it to consult my Errands context in the Toodledo app (to see what I can get done while I'm out) and to check my calendar and schedule appointments.

After Work/School

My Bullet Journal accompanies me from my office to the family/common areas of our home. It typically lives on the dining room table or the kitchen counter. I consult the Daily Log again to make sure I'm on track to finish my tasks for the day. Some, like gathering and taking out the trash the night before collection day, can be delegated to others during this time.

If I continue working on writing projects or planning, I try to do this in my Bullet Journal, not on a computer. This helps me mentally and allows me to doodle if I need to, but it also sets an example for my family regarding screen time.

Evening

I take one last look at the day's schedule. Did I forget to do anything? (This is where I usually realize I haven't put the trash out at the curb.) Have I acknowledged any birthdays or anniversaries that fall on that day? What's happening tomorrow that I may need to prepare for?

I plug in my phone in the kitchen (not in the bedroom!). Then, I leave my Bullet Journal open on the table for the morning, when we'll start all over again.

BULLET JOURNAL & GTD

It's important to note here that my entire organizing system is built on GTD. My GTD system feeds my Bullet Journal, not the other way around, and I don't use the Bullet Journal as a standalone system. Most people's lives, mine included, are too complicated for a Bullet Journal to cover everything.

However, if you do adopt a pen-and-paper system for keeping track of your tasks, projects, and calendar, I highly recommend you organize it in a Bullet Journal. The reason is indexing.

The most important rule of Bullet Journaling is this: always add new content to the index *before* you start writing on the page. When I start a grocery list, I first write the page number in the index at the front of my notebook. *Then* I write my list. In a Bullet Journal, every shred of content is cataloged in the index, just like your favorite reference book, so you can find it later.

This also makes it easy to spread content in a single category across your entire notebook without losing the thread. For example, here are a few index entries from my Bullet Journal:

Figure 10 *Bullet Journal Index Entries*

My Bullet Journal is part diary, part to-do-list, part filing system, part calendar. Some of this content comes to the notebook via a one-way street. Specifically, anything from my calendar or task lists. The Bullet Journal is a reflection of my Google Calendar and Toodle-do systems, distilled onto a handwritten page. This allows me to choose what goes into the Daily Log and to eliminate non-urgent distractions. However, I still appreciate the powerful tools Google Calendar and Toodledo bring to the table. To figure out what works best for you, you'll have to assess how much you have going on and how you want to keep track of it. Most of us will benefit from electronic tools even if we also use a paper notebook.

BULLET JOURNAL & MINI HABITS

A bit later in this book, I'll introduce you to mini habits, from a book of the same name by Stephen Guise. For now, the gist of it is this: mini habits are small (smaller than you think) things you do daily to form larger positive habits. Guise began his own mini habits journey with a resolution to do one push-up every day. This small act grew into a new healthy lifestyle.[52]

I generally track 1–3 mini habits at any given time. When I'm drafting a new book, I also track my daily word count. You can see this in Figure 11, which shows a daily log from the writing of this book. "OFC WC" refers to the number of new words I wrote that day. You'll also notice I'm tracking music practice (picking up and playing one instrument every day, even if it's only one note or chord) and yoga (one pose per day).

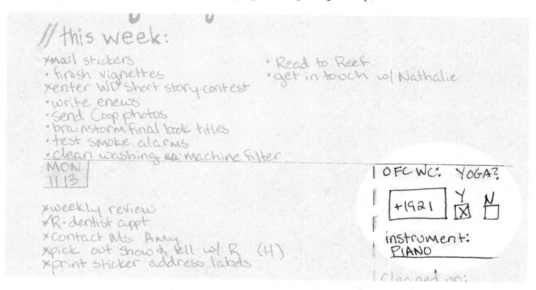

Figure 11 Bullet Journal Mini Habit

I used to keep a record of mini habits in a checklist by my bed, but I now track them right in my Daily Log. I began doing this after I switched from the lined Moleskine notebook to the dotted version, because the dots make it easier to separate information into boxes and columns.

Because my Bullet Journal greets me at the breakfast table each morning and travels everywhere with me throughout the day, I have frequent reminders of my personal goals.

---

52 (Guise, 2013)

KEY TAKEAWAYS

- Unlike apps or store-bought planners, Bullet Journals can be completely customized to suit the user.

- A Bullet Journal can organize information offline, away from smart phone distractions.

- The most important part of the Bullet Journal is its index.

- Writing information by hand can help some people think it through and remember more effectively.

PUTTING IT ALL TOGETHER: MY ORGANIZING TOOLBOX

Now that we've explored the organizing tools individually, let's zoom out. Equipped with a well-stocked organizing toolbox, full of tools hand-picked for you and your brain, you can bring it all together into a cohesive system.

Here's a look at my organizing and productivity routines and how they fit into the big picture of my life.

DAILY

Each day, I have four primary responsibilities related to keeping myself organized:

- Manage new items flowing into my inboxes.
- Complete time-bound tasks.
- Attend or acknowledge important events and appointments for the day.
- Complete any to-do items I can from my Next Actions list *after* the time-bound tasks are complete.

Here's how that looks over the course of the day:

Morning (First Thing):

- Wake up and make breakfast.
- Consult Daily Log to remind myself of any appointments/time commitments.
- Take meds.
- See the rest of the family off to school/work.
- Once the house is quiet, go through my email and physical inboxes.
- Look at Daily Log again and start any tasks that need to be done today.

Late Morning/Early Afternoon:

- After making sure must-do-today tasks are under control, consult Next Actions list and consider my context(s) before working on tasks in these contexts:
  - Desktop (Office) Computer.
  - Phone (Talking).
  - House (While child is asleep/away).
- Take occasional breaks to process emails as they come in.

Late Afternoon:

- Pick my son up from school; spend time with him if he's interested, consult Next Actions if he has his own thing to do, and follow his lead on where to hang out. Work on tasks in the following contexts:
  - House (Anytime, i.e. child can be around for these tasks).
  - Tasks I need to do with my son.
  - Outdoors.
  - Phone (Texting).
  - Basement/Craft Room.
- Collect mail from mailbox; put any obvious junk mail into the recycling and dump the rest into my inbox by the front door.

Evening:

- Cook dinner.
- Clean kitchen, remind my son to clean up anything he's gotten out.
- Help my son get ready for bed.
- After my son is in bed, relax! Or, if I have it in me to do something else, look for Next Actions that avoid sitting at a computer:
  - House (While child is asleep/away).
  - Basement/Craft Room.
  - Television (i.e. these tasks can be done in front of the TV).

EVERY 2-3 DAYS

While I strive to reach Inbox Zero every day, I'm going to be real here: it rarely happens. While I may eventually get there by unsubscribing from or blocking a few recurring emails, for now I'm okay with emptying those inboxes every few days. If I let things go for a full week, I start to feel stressed. I worry I'll miss something important or put myself in a bind with a deadline. Every few days, I make sure my email and physical inboxes are empty. This is critical to making my Weekly Review (which I'll explain shortly) feel manageable. Otherwise it takes too long and I put it off (or don't finish it at all).

I also look over my "this week" section of the Daily Log every few days. These are tasks that must be done this week, but don't have a specific day attached to them. While I shouldn't try to knock them all out on Monday morning, neither should I run around panicking over this list on Friday afternoon. A regular glance over the list reminds me to do them as I'm able.

WEEKLY

I begin every week with something called a Weekly Review. Without it, I'm unable to conceptualize what I need to accomplish over the next seven days. The Weekly Review is when I review all my lists, projects, and calendars. It prompts me to look over my system as a whole to ensure all parts are functioning, and to make sure my inboxes and recurring tasks are all current.

David Allen describes the Weekly Review as the "master key" to maintaining a complete organizational system that you trust — and need — enough to maintain and keep current.[53] Without the Weekly Review, I'd still have my calendar and my list of Next Actions. I'd still create new projects in Toodledo. But I'd lose the big picture. For those with ADHD especially, the big picture must be tangible. Otherwise we cannot grasp what has been done or what we still need to do. Something will slip through the cracks.

My Weekly Review has evolved over the years. While everyone should make a point of reviewing their calendar, open projects, and Next Actions/to-do list every week, you may want to add more items to suit your needs. I kick off every Monday morning with my Weekly Review. Here's what it looks like:

GTD-Related Tasks:

- Make sure all inboxes are empty.
- Review my loose ends and follow up as necessary on:
    - @Waiting label in Gmail.
    - Waiting folder in my desk's file drawer.
    - Tasks with a Waiting status in Toodledo.
- Review my calendar:
    - Take a look at my Bullet Journal's Monthly Log to make sure I'm on track.
    - Glance over last week's Daily Log to catch anything I missed.
    - Create a new Daily Log and add it to the Bullet Journal index, then populate it with events, tasks, and reminders from Google Calendar.
- Review Toodledo Next Actions list:
    - Check off any tasks I completed but forgot to mark as such.
    - Delete any tasks that aren't associated with a project, aren't truly necessary, and probably won't get done.
- Review Someday Maybe list.
- Review list of Projects and make sure each one has a Next Action listed.

---

53 (Allen, 2015)

My Additions:

- Open our online banking account and make sure everything looks good:
    - Online bill pay is up to date and scheduled to automatically pay any bills coming due soon.
    - Checking account has enough funds to cover all scheduled transactions/bill payments.
    - Transactions in all accounts are up to date in my budgeting app (If you don't have one yet, I recommend You Need a Budget).
- Log into our online credit card accounts and make sure all transactions have been entered into our budgeting app.
- Clean off my desk, removing clutter from the physical one in front of me and moving files from my computer's Desktop to their proper homes in my file system.
- Review my blogs' publication calendars, rearrange as necessary, then schedule tasks to make sure posts will go live on schedule.
- Schedule my next Weekly Review on my Google Calendar so I won't forget it.

You may wonder how I keep track of all this. I don't. I have a checklist in Google's Keep app, and I refer to it every single week. As I finish one part of my Weekly Review, I check it off. This way, nothing gets forgotten and I won't lose my place if I have to take a break in the middle. You don't need an app for this. I use one because I travel frequently enough, I need to be able to do a modified Weekly Review on the road at times. You can use a small dry erase board, a printed checklist, or a list written on a piece of notebook paper. The key is to assume you will forget any or all steps in your Weekly Review unless you write them down.

You may also wonder how I make time for all of this. I have several answers to that question. First and foremost, I've learned — sometimes the hard way — that I feel incredibly anxious if I skip the Weekly Review. This is my time to collect my thoughts, review the upcoming week, and make sure I'm not about to be blindsided by a key responsibility or deadline I've forgotten. This makes the Weekly Review a priority because I've grown to rely on it.

However, I won't do it just because it's necessary and neither will you. I'm willing to spend the first hour in my office every Monday on this review. I'm willing to sandwich it piecemeal between activities on a family vacation. I'm not willing to make it a guaranteed all-day ordeal.

To that end, I make sure the Weekly Review goes as quickly as possible. First, you'll notice I mentioned doing it in the morning. I can do my Review any time, but there's one nonnegotiable requirement: my meds must be in effect. Without meds, I get too distracted, too caught up in doing all the things instead of reviewing all the things, and the Review takes an impractically long time — if I can force myself to do it at all. You need to learn when your brain functions best and schedule your weekly review for that time slot.

I also keep my Weekly Review rather lean by doing maintenance during the week. My Monday-morning Weekly Review isn't an appropriate time to catch up on a week's worth of procrastination. That will only make it intimidating and unapproachable. Here are a few tips for a quick and easy Weekly Review:

- **As soon as you receive a bill**, log into your online banking account and schedule it to be paid (or write a check and stick it in the envelope). If it's going to overdraw the checking account, schedule a transfer from savings right then and there.
- **Always ask for receipts** when you buy something at a store. These go into the inbox to be recorded in a budgeting app. (You can also use a budgeting app that imports transactions automatically.)
- **Keep inboxes from getting bloated**. Empty them every 2-3 days so the task doesn't feel overwhelming. Again, sit down to do this when your brain is at its peak effectiveness because emptying inboxes is almost always tedious and unappealing.
- If any of this regular maintenance becomes a consistent stumbling block, **create a mini habit to make it more approachable** (more on mini habits under *Rule #4*).
- **Cut down on the number of projects you have going at once**. Move some to your Someday Maybe list or find a way to let them go entirely.
- **Read** *Rule #4* in this book and be ruthless about sticking to it.

YOUR SYSTEM MUST BE SUSTAINABLE

If you're afraid this system will fall apart on you at some point, you're probably right. This has happened to me, and I bet it'll happen to you. The reasons are many: maybe you've spent more days out of town than at home this month. Maybe you're getting a new book out the door and everything else has to take a back seat. Maybe you're off your meds because you're trying to get pregnant. Maybe your pharmacy switched you to a different generic medication and the effectiveness isn't the same. Maybe there's nothing dramatic afoot, your kids have just had 16 snow days since Christmas and you feel like you haven't had a normal day in six weeks. No system is bulletproof, especially for someone with ADHD.

When I say a system must be sustainable, I don't mean it needs to be impervious to failure. It does, however, need to be something you can sustain under normal conditions and reassemble with minimal help when it breaks down. Occasional failures will teach you valuable lessons about what needs to change or improve. Daily, relentless failures will overwhelm you and make you feel like you shouldn't even try. Aim for the former, not the latter.

Remember my story about going back on ADHD meds after my son was born? How I knew something was wrong when I stopped doing my Weekly Review? My Weekly Review is my lifeline. I make myself do it, just like I make myself go to the grocery store every week. I don't enjoy either of these chores, but they enable me to reap big rewards through-out the week — big enough that I wouldn't consider skipping them. Identify red flags that signal bigger problems for you and keep a close eye on them.

When your system is running like a well-oiled machine, you're emptying your inbox and dealing with everything on a regular basis. You are *not* dumping all your filing into a pile to file later. As a person with ADHD, I recommend you avoid terms like "soon" and "later," as their value tends to shift based on your motivation to complete a task.

When I pull a piece of filing from my inbox, I file it. Done. If this isn't possible for some reason, that indicates a flaw in my system. Am I letting my inbox get too full before I get around to emptying it? Am I getting too much junk mail? Can I sign up for e-statements from my bank? Am I the person who should be doing all this filing, or can my spouse share some of the burden? Or maybe I've set up my office wrong. Do I have to leave the room to find the labelmaker? Am I out of file folders? These are all specific issues I can solve to get my system running again, rather than create a to-file pile that will languish on my office floor for the next two years.

Bottom line: after you clear your initial backlog, your organizing system — whatever it ends up looking like — should be able to handle your typical inflow. You should not have to put aside filing to do later as its own separate task after you process your inbox. When you bring home a bag from the store, you should be able to empty it immediately rather than leaving it sitting on your dining room table for two weeks. Your things should be put away and under control enough that you can clean your house and keep it healthy for you and your family. If you find yourself back in the morass of clutter, filing piles, and random shopping bags on the dining room table, it's time to re-assess your system. You either need to tweak your process, reduce the amount of stuff coming in, or perhaps even tweak your *meds* if a previously excellent system is crumbling with no external reason.

KEY TAKEAWAYS

- Use a Weekly Review to look over your loose ends, projects, to-do lists, calendars, upcoming bills, etc. and begin each week with a clean slate.

- A checklist will help you remember everything you need to do during your Weekly Review.

- If your Weekly Review takes too long, you won't do it.

- Reduce the length of your Weekly Review by eliminating excess projects and doing more maintenance during the week.

- Make sure your system is sustainable for the long term by keeping your Weekly Review short and manageable, getting your ADHD symptoms under control, and giving yourself a workspace that meets your needs.

BUT IT WON'T WORK FOR ME...

At this point in the book, I'd be willing to bet some of you are feeling amped. Organizational systems have regained their shiny novelty for you. You can't wait to hop online and order a bunch of supplies or download the apps I've suggested.

Others, not so much. You've been burned before and you think you'll be burned again. This all sounds great, you say, but none of this stuff ever works.

If you're hesitating, or returning to this book after a previous failure, take a look at the writing exercise below. Copy the template onto a fresh piece of paper and make a list of all the roadblocks you've encountered in the past.

Remember to be objective. Pretend you're troubleshooting a broken-down car or a computer program. Your goal is to fix something that's broken, not make character judgements and tear yourself down.

WRITING EXERCISE: TROUBLESHOOTING YOUR SYSTEM

Remember the first chapter of this section, *Be Agile*? Now's the time to think through all you've learned, look at what's failed for you in the past, and craft your very own organizational system. Here are some examples to get you started.

Failed organizational tool/system:
Inbox (physical).

What's happening?
Inbox always fills to overflowing. I never empty it, so important stuff gets buried. If something really matters, I tape it to my computer monitor or give it to my spouse to take care of because I don't trust myself.

Why might this be happening?
When I get home from work, this is the absolute last thing I want to do. I just can't seem to make myself do it. My spouse has taken over everything urgent because she doesn't trust me to get it done, so there are fewer consequences for slacking off.

What could I try instead?
Set a low goal at first, and change the time of day. Process one, and only one, item out of my inbox each morning before I leave for work. Allow these small successes to snowball, but keep the pressure low for now. Take items back from my spouse gradually, and only after the inbox gets under control.

Failed organizational tool/system:
Cleaning the house on a reasonable schedule.

What's happening?
I would love to invite my friends and colleagues over for dinner, but it feels like such a project. When I do have to entertain, I stress about it for a week beforehand and I spend an hour and a half scrubbing our tiny bathroom because it's gotten so filthy.

Why might this be happening?
While I do avoid cleaning the bathroom sometimes, the real issue is I just don't think of it when I have the time and energy to do it. I remember when I'm in there, and forget by the time I'm all the way out the door.

What could I try instead?
Keep cleaning supplies under every sink in the house. Use disposable bathroom wipes even though I hate them. Give things a two-minute wipe-down as soon as I notice they're getting dirty. When it's time for a deeper clean, write it on my to-do list in the appropriate context (e.g. "at home, high physical energy").

Use this format to write your own list of issues to troubleshoot.

Notice the most important aspect of this exercise: you're not trying to change *yourself*, you're trying to change your *system*. Many of us tell ourselves, "but I should be able to handle this," when "this" is something we've reliably *not* handled for our entire adult lives.

It's much easier to change your strategy than to change your brain. There's no glory in trying yet again to succeed at something you've failed to do 100 times before. If your car doesn't start, you figure out why and you fix it. Perhaps you try turning the key a few more times because you're convinced it really *should* be doing a better job at being a car. Hopefully it doesn't take you long to realize this isn't going to solve the problem. Apply this same approach to a bathroom that doesn't get clean and you'll start to see a little more progress.

KEY TAKEAWAYS

- It's much easier to change your system than it is to change yourself.

- Don't judge yourself for failures; write the problem down and troubleshoot solutions instead.

RULE #4:
STRIVE FOR LESS
(STUFF, DISTRACTION, AND
OVERWHELM)

THE PURSUIT OF LESS

ADHD makes it difficult to manage our lives. We know this. But there are two sides to the story, and most of us can't blame all our organizing woes on our brains. At least not in the way we think.

My first *ADHD Homestead* post about time blindness has been a standout with readers since I published it in 2015. One reader left a particularly insightful comment for me:

> I need a lot of time where I don't have anything scheduled or planned [in order to] cope with the times there is a lot more pressure on me. My anxiety is too severe and I get too worn out by having to constantly cope with outside pressures…I need uninterrupted down time to lose track of time as a rest period. I cope a lot better with time management when I have these times regularly.

Sound familiar? Down time can be elusive for many of us with ADHD. For my entire life, I've self-medicated by taking on too much and over-structuring my life. I struggle to give myself any time to relax because I don't know how to settle down. Only in recent years have I learned to take a true vacation, where I don't pack any projects or work and I allow myself to have at least some time that's not scheduled in advance.

This commenter hits on a key point for everyone, especially adults with ADHD: we need to give ourselves space to breathe. If you're struggling to get organized or stay on top of your basic responsibilities, don't be too quick to blame it on a defective brain or lack of organizing skills — or at the very least don't cite that as the *only* reason. It's possible that even on your best day, with a full pot of coffee and the perfect organizing toolbox, you're asking yourself to manage too much.

Because we're drawn to novelty, because we crave stimulation, and because we lack a firm grasp on time itself, people with ADHD have trouble saying no. We aren't very good at assessing our lives and saying, "this is enough," or even more difficult, "this is too much." For those of us who have self-medicated and motivated ourselves with a workaholic lifestyle, saying "enough" (let alone "too much") flies in the face of our very identity. For many, too much feels like not enough.

With this in mind, take a moment before reading much further to reassess your symptom management. Living life on overload is often an indication of poorly managed ADHD. Proper symptom management will go a long way to making the idea of less feel palatable. When I first started taking stimulant medication for my ADHD, some of these issues even self-corrected. I noticed myself drinking a heck of a lot less because I no longer felt a need to maintain a certain level of buzz to enjoy a social gathering. I stopped drinking sugary cocktails entirely and the idea of being *drunk* became completely undesirable. I ate less, too. I still enjoyed outdoor recreation, like downhill skiing, but I stopped taking stupid risks. I no longer enjoyed driving fast or turning the radio up crazy loud. For the first time, too much actually felt like…too much.

The things we own, what we put into our bodies, which sights and sounds we prefer, the goals we set and the jobs we hold: all of these can become a form of self-medication. We can seek too much in a subconscious effort to raise the baseline for an understimulated brain. This is why — ironically, considering its reputation in popular culture — stimulant medication works. It makes more dopamine available to the brain in the first place, reducing our craving to find that stimulation somewhere else.

Until you've gotten these cravings and stimulation-seeking behaviors under control, you'll probably struggle with too much of something in your life. If that comes in the form of activities, obligations, projects, or stuff, you'll have a very difficult time getting and staying organized.

Remember what I said about hyperfocus being a kind of addiction for some people? Overstimulation can work the same way. Starting a new project — that magical moment when it all begins — *feels good* to me. It feels good in a way my brain doesn't want to give up. Continuing work on a project until it's done? That has proven to be an acquired taste.

As I've learned to manage my ADHD in ways that serve my long-term mental and physical health, I've learned to thrive with less. I've worked hard to let go of my desire for more stuff, for overambitious goals, for starting every project the moment I think of it. I've learned that the less I have in my life, both physically and mentally, the better I am at keeping it all under control.

Big surprise, right?

Like the blog commenter said, it's easier to manage high-pressure situations when you're not maxed out on a normal day. It's a lot like keeping an emergency buffer in your bank account. Everyone has unexpected expenses come up and everyone makes a big impulse purchase at least once in their lives. If you're living hand to mouth, you leave yourself unable to absorb the challenges life throws your way. Sometimes you don't even have enough to cover the basics. I've always loved to live below my financial means. However, doing it with my time and energy has required more effort.

In this final section, I'm going to share some of my most valuable lessons on thriving with less and giving myself space to be me. And that's the real me, not the me I want people to see on Instagram or Pinterest. The real me needs a wide margin of error, and that can only be achieved through a more minimalist approach to life.

KEY TAKEAWAYS

- ADHD leads us to seek additional stimulation. Sometimes we find this stimulation by overscheduling ourselves, starting one new project after another, or collecting too much stuff.

- Out-of-control ADHD symptoms may make it impossible for you to get and stay organized.

- If we live every day feeling maxed out, we won't have energy to deal with unexpected challenges.

- If you give yourself breathing room with your schedule and obligations, you give yourself freedom to make mistakes without catastrophic consequences.

LESS PRESSURE (LOWER YOUR EXPECTATIONS)

In *Mini Habits: Smaller Habits, Bigger Results*, Stephen Guise encourages readers to reject motivation as a strategy to get anywhere.[54] If you believe you need to feel motivated in order to do something, you have a perfect excuse to avoid doing what you're supposed to do.

Guise insists that to develop long-term habits, we need to rely on willpower, not feeling motivated or inspired.[55] And yet willpower is a finite resource, so we need to use as little as possible to achieve success. Enter Mini Habits: a tiny version — "stupid small," as Guise puts it — of the habit you want to form. For example, setting a goal of one push-up per day, not 100.

The Mini Habits concept is especially important for people with ADHD not just because we suffer from inertia, but because so many of us have limited experience with success. During one of my many protracted attempts to repaint our home, I found myself struggling with the dining room. It had spent several weeks half-prepped for paint and now sat spackled, but not sanded. These situations cause us ADHDers particular anguish because

---

54 (Guise, 2013)
55 (Guise, 2013)

we see our friends spend a weekend repainting their entire downstairs and cannot understand why it takes us months or years to do the same. Our failure snowballs, along with our negative feelings about the entire project.

When I found myself sinking into this quagmire once again, I realized I needed to lower my bar for success. I told myself I only had to touch the piece of wet sandpaper to the wall one time, in one spot, to call that day a success. I wouldn't have wanted to admit this to anyone. Not only was the goal itself pathetic, I had no explanation for how it would lead to a painted dining room in under two years.

And yet it did. I had set expectations so low, *even a person with ADHD could not avoid the task*. This takes some doing. But even if I desperately wanted to procrastinate, surely I could wet a piece of sandpaper and touch it to the wall, couldn't I? And once I was there, the ADHD inertia worked to my advantage. I didn't finish the job in one day, and sometimes I didn't work for very long, but I kept going. After a few days, my dining room was ready for a new coat of paint.

My biggest reward was not a nice dining room, but the simple fact that it had happened at all. Many people with ADHD resign ourselves to a home full of half-finished projects. We don't know what it feels like to win, let alone how to advance toward the finish line. I didn't even care what my dining room looked like. All I could think about was my realization that *I could do this.*

Once you experience one success, you may have an easier time convincing yourself it could happen again. This is not a time for heroism. Don't set out to complete a big project in a weekend. Commit instead to doing an embarrassingly small amount — really, just enough to ensure you have some interaction with your goal — every day. Lofty goals, if I give them time, almost always kill my motivation and self-esteem. Tiny, daily acts deliver surprises in the form of accomplishments I previously thought impossible.

I often include Mini-Habit-style goals in my Bullet Journal's Daily Log. When I feel my home slipping into disarray, I commit to cleaning up *one thing* every day. This can be as simple as carrying a tape dispenser back to my office — something I still struggle to believe can lead to bigger results. But by the end of the week, I always feel much more organized and in control.

ADHD VS. LONG-TERM CHANGE

After reading *Mini Habits*, my husband tried the one-pushup challenge. It did not transform his life as it did Guise's, nor did it mark the beginning of a long-term fitness habit. As with almost every new good habit people with ADHD begin, it eventually faded into his distant memory.

That doesn't mean he failed. Guise presents Mini Habits as a gateway to major, long-term lifestyle shifts. This may or may not be realistic for people with ADHD. But Mini Habits can change the way we think about large undertakings and make project completion and new habits accessible when they were previously out of reach.

My husband stuck with his daily push-ups for longer than he's stuck with any new habit. There is a huge difference between not being able to stay upright on a bike at all and being able to ride for 20 yards before falling off. As someone who's learned several balance-intensive sports, I think that first feeling of "I'm doing it! I'm doing it!" gives you the keys to the world. It's like getting that manual-transmission car moving for the first time instead of stalling right away. You learn what it's supposed to feel like, and it's a thrill akin to flying. You may later decide it's not worth it to keep learning to snowboard, drive a stick shift, or ride a unicycle. But that fleeting moment, your first taste of success, lets you hold the prize in your own two hands. It becomes a real thing, and maybe a thrill you want to keep chasing.

Remember that dopamine fuels our desire. People with ADHD struggle with that desire. Our logical brains know we want rewards (even if they're simply the absence of a negative, e.g. not letting the car run out of gas), but ADHD cripples our ability to work for them. We gravitate toward anything that provides quick, repeated bursts of dopamine (Facebook, Doritos, making inappropriate jokes) and avoid doing boring work in service of long-term goals.

When you lower the bar for success, you remove your important goals from the category of big, adult responsibilities you've never been good at. You move them closer to an eating-Doritos level of effort and associate them with pleasant rewards rather than shame and avoidance.

In short, while I admire the changes Guise and others have made in their lives using Mini Habits, it's important to remember it's not a pass/fail course. Making progress possible doesn't guarantee permanent, uninterrupted results. Mini Habits didn't teach me that I'm able to maintain an unbroken daily yoga practice for the rest of my life. I'm not. But I can restart that habit with very little effort. I've ensured the climb back onto the wagon will be neither long nor strenuous.

Don't be afraid to try a Mini Habit for a week, with no expectations. Use this concept to change the way you think about both projects and habits. When you feel stuck, ask yourself to do the smallest possible thing. If you still resist, make it even smaller. Don't clean the whole sink. Wash one fork. Once you have the soap out, maybe you'll wash a bowl, too. Or maybe you won't, and that'll be okay. Watch your miniscule progress grow into something more, and use that as evidence that yes, you can do this.

Whatever you do, even if you experience a huge success, don't expect *this* to be the time your positive changes finally last. That mentality will set you up for disappointment when something inevitably throws a wrench in the works. Instead, take what you've learned — smaller is better when it comes to favors you ask of yourself — and use it to build a good life at a reasonable pace. And when you do get tripped up, take small steps to get things back in order as opposed to attacking the situation with unsustainable gusto.

KEY TAKEAWAYS

- Let go of lofty goals that sound impressive to tell your friends. They'll only chip away at your self-esteem when you fail to achieve them.

- Set tiny daily goals that require almost no effort. For example, pick up one item from your living room and put it away.

- When you do experience success, savor it! But don't assume life will be easy from then on or allow yourself to feel discouraged when you mess up again. Life happens.

LESS TO DO

Most adults have a calendar full of weekly or monthly commitments that we take for grant-ed. We have game nights, PTA meetings, happy hours, and book clubs. We have television shows we watch as soon as they air. These events have been in our lives so long, we don't even think about them. But they all take time, and time is something we all feel desperate for more of.

Think about it: how many times have you lamented that if only you had an entire day, an entire weekend, with no distractions, you could catch up on everything you've allowed to pile up? How often has your email inbox ballooned to thousands of unread messages, and you found yourself waiting for that mystical time when you had a few free hours to get through it all? How many times has your house grown dirty and cluttered because you couldn't seem to find the time to clean?

Sure, we all need to learn to give ourselves a kick in the pants from time to time. But we also need to be ruthless with our time and attention. People with ADHD have trouble say-ing no. If it sounds fun, how can we resist? Especially when we're forgetting all the other responsibilities lurking in the background? Pretty soon, we're saddled with more than we can handle.

Rule #1: accept your reality. Even if your best friend manages to juggle a full social schedule, a demanding career, and several volunteer commitments, that lifestyle may not be possible for you. As I've gotten older, I've made peace with the fact that my ADHD makes me work harder. I need to spend more time organizing my life and setting myself up for success. I can't hold it all — or much of anything, really — in my head. Professional and social relationships take real work. If I try to maintain too many, they all suffer and I end up feeling drained and guilty. As a person with ADHD, you need to take commitments seriously and refuse to enter into them lightly — even if someone else is telling you otherwise.

If you're feeling overwhelmed, pare back, even if it's temporary. You don't need to quit everything for good. When I committed to editing a novel in advance of a writers' conference where I could pitch the story to literary agents, I knew I needed to make more time in my life. I did this in part by taking a long hiatus from a book club I very much enjoyed. While I valued the social connections it provided, the book selection process at the time had given me several duds. It wasn't just the time I spent meeting with the book club every month, it was the hours I spent reading books that weren't contributing value to my life. At a time when I felt a lot of pressure to finish my novel, I had to let go of several activities to make room. When I completed this work, I added back some of the activities I'd cut.

WRITING EXERCISE: WHO AM I?

Sit down in a quiet place and list all the roles you play, in your life and in others'. I am a wife, mother, sister, fiction writer, friend, blogger, homeowner, and community volunteer, just to name a few.

Next, rank these roles in terms of how they relate to your Why. Which are near and dear, and which roles do you hold onto because you (or someone else) think you should? Which take up the most time? Which get lost in the shuffle and burden you with guilt?

Now think about the roles that fail to resonate with your Why. Be honest about your commitment to these roles and brainstorm a few you could — ethically, of course — part with to make room for your true priorities.

This is like the "Let It Go" writing exercise under *Rule #1*, but bigger. While at the beginning of this journey you identified projects, tasks, and commitments to let go, now you may feel empowered to release entire roles from your life. For example, maybe you've been coaching a local soccer team since your kids played as children, but they've all gone off to college. Passing the baton would require you to let go of your identity as a sports coach, but it would also make room for you to strengthen other roles in your life. Which is more important?

DOING LESS DOES NOT MEAN ADMITTING FAILURE

Let's be forthright about something here: when we say "no" or "I can't," many of us feel like we're admitting failure. We should be able to do it all, but we can't. People with ADHD may be especially familiar with the feeling of letting others down and especially hesitant to do it voluntarily.

You need to let that go. Failing to follow through on a promise? Never having time for your family? Dropping the ball on a big project at work? That's letting people down. Think about the last time someone told you, "I'm sorry, that sounds like a great opportunity, but I can't take on anything new right now." The people I respect — and envy — the most are masters at saying no, and they aren't afraid to step down from a role if it doesn't serve their Why.

Gracefully and responsibly lightening your load doesn't make you look weak, incapable, or unambitious. Sure, you may disappoint people along the way, and these choices will be difficult. But you will define yourself as a person who knows who you are and what you want. You will show others that you have deeply held values and you protect what's important to you.

I used to play the popular online role-playing game World of Warcraft, where I was a member of a small guild (a group of players who share resources and play together). It was a misfit band of LGBT-identified-or-friendly nerds, most of whose real names I didn't know. I spent hours completing group challenges and shooting the breeze in our guild chat. We hosted weekly raid nights, where I was known for being a skilled player in my role. In other words, this was more than just a game: it was a social group unto itself, every bit as legitimate as those I met in real life, and it was a place where I felt competent and valued.

Then my life changed. I quit my job. I decided to get serious about my writing career. I had a child and assumed full-time caregiving responsibilities. For a while, I kept playing World of Warcraft.

Then I took a hard look at the time I spent gaming. I valued my identity as a female gamer — married with a child, no less — and felt I would lose something by giving it up. I had no way to connect with the people in my guild outside the game and I didn't want to say goodbye to my friends there. And yet gaming wasn't my future. Writing was.

I vowed to cancel my subscription until I'd finished my novel and built my blog into a successful business. Almost five years later, I still miss it. I've told myself I'll go back if I ever feel I have the time. For now, I need to focus on selling my completed novel manuscript and building *The ADHD Homestead* into the best resource it can be.

Trivial though it may seem, this was a difficult choice for me. I had to give up a piece of my identity and say goodbye to a social group I cared about. I miss gaming, and I feel left out when friends talk about the latest games. But I decided to prioritize my writing career and give myself the best chance of success. For some, gaming plays a bigger role in personal identity or social activities, or a day job provides a sufficient outlet for professional goals. I had to sacrifice this part of my life to serve my Why.

Will you have to make some uncomfortable sacrifices? Probably. You may have to prioritize your hobbies, cut out a side hustle, or quit your book club. This doesn't make you a less interesting person or a bad friend. In fact, you may find people paying more attention and giving you more respect when you deepen your commitments rather than casting an impossibly wide net.

KEY TAKEAWAYS

- Even if others around you appear to juggle an impossible number of personal and professional commitments, that doesn't make it the right choice for you.

- Just like you've pared down projects, tasks, and commitments that don't serve your Why, you may need to take a hard look at the roles you play — even ones you consider part of your personal identity.

- Saying no or letting go isn't the same as admitting defeat.

- When you gain the confidence to say no more often and save your time for what matters most, you may find you earn more respect from others as well.

LESS HOUSE TO CLEAN AND MAINTAIN

I grew up in a traditional 1300-square-foot, three-bedroom home. The four of us shared one living room, one dining room, a kitchen, one-and-a-half bathrooms, and a finished basement. No private bathrooms, no formal living room, no rooms we only used on special occasions.

You might think that when I got married and had a child of my own, I would buy a larger house if we could afford it. This is not the case. I live in a home very similar in size and configuration to the one I grew up in, and that feels like plenty for me. Sometimes it feels like too much. When I spend time at a family vacation home — a two-bedroom bungalow — cleaning the place feels downright luxurious.

Unfortunately, many of us seek to display our status to others through our homes' size and amenities. As we move through our adult lives, we assume we should purchase the biggest and best house we can. We ask our mortgage broker for the magic number: how much can I afford? The amount of our pre-approved loan dictates which houses we can look at, which neighborhood we can live in, and how much pride and excitement we can feel about hosting Thanksgiving. Why would we go for less?

If we enjoy a certain level of success, we start looking for extras: features that cater toward guests, or amenities that aren't necessary to our family's daily life. We strive for grand entryways, fancy landscaping along a seldom-used front walk, a pool, a formal living room. We invest a small fortune in a new kitchen, even if we don't like to cook. If we have these things, we take pride in them. If we lack them, we covet them.

Paradoxically, our homes can be a major source of stress: we struggle to keep up with cleaning, repairs, curb appeal, and mortgage payments. Maintaining our homes makes us feel like successful adults. Living in a messy home or keeping an untidy front yard makes us wary of others' judgement.

We should, of course, strive to do better and to maintain our homes to the best of our ability. But we need to reexamine our need for *more*.

My family lives in a modest rowhome in a lovely Baltimore neighborhood. We've made great friends here and watched a block full of children grow from infancy to school age. A few families have left for more house, more yard, more suburban amenities. Some of those families I have not heard from. Others return for our annual block party because their new community lacks such a thing. Still others express longing for what they left behind and have begun scanning real estate listings in hope of returning.

If we ever seriously consider buying a bigger house, I'll demand a good reason, like providing a home for aging parents. And I want certain conditions to be met before we move. I want us to be using 100 percent of our current home's space effectively. No clutter, no abandoned boxes of college textbooks, no messy closets, no possessions we could easily live without. I want to have proven empirically that we *need* more space.

Because more space always means more responsibility. Everything in this book becomes more difficult to accomplish as you scale up. A bigger house and/or a bigger yard bring more time spent cleaning, more spaces to police for clutter, and more potential maintenance issues. People with ADHD struggle to get things done. We struggle to stay on top of household chores, and these struggles often lead to marital strife. The fewer such responsibilities you can create for yourself, the better. The more time and energy you will have for the things (and people) you value the most.

Task execution and home maintenance are only the tip of the iceberg for many adults with ADHD. Many of us also struggle to keep on top of our finances. Few people with ADHD get excited about sitting down to create a budget, much less follow one. Impulsive spending undermines what long-term financial plans we do have. In short, too many adults with ADHD live with financial insecurity.

I'm not an accountant, but I know this much: my husband and I are on track to be mortgage-free by the time our son graduates from middle school. We don't need to pay someone to clean our house. If the impulse shopper among us has a late-night affair with Amazon Prime, we have a buffer. No spending misstep has ever started a fight over how we'll pay our bills at the end of the month.

Certainly, ADHDers need to learn restraint and accountability. We need to maintain our homes at a basic level and resist buying everything that excites us in the moment.

But we also need space to be compassionate with ourselves. If you live below your means, if you don't spend every dollar before you've even made it, it gives you freedom. Freedom to reign in that spending habit without ruining your credit or alienating your spouse. Freedom to shop around for someone who will do a top-quality repair job when your roof leaks. Freedom to make those inevitable mistakes on your way to self-improvement with a little less pressure.

Freedom to lead a calm, uncluttered, and grateful life. When you let go of your need for more house, you may find yourself with more of everything else.

KEY TAKEAWAYS

- The bigger your house and yard, the more difficult everything outlined in this book becomes.

- If you take on the biggest mortgage loan you can afford, you have less room each month to make mistakes with impulse purchases.

- People with ADHD usually struggle to keep up with household chores, and a smaller house makes those chores more approachable.

- If you think you need a bigger house, start by clearing all the clutter from the house you have.

- Your house should be a clean, healthy, and inviting space for your family to live — not a status symbol.

LESS TO CLEAN AROUND

Here's a little fact I've had to accept. File it under *Rule #1: You Must Make Peace With Reality.*

If I have to move stuff out of the way to clean something, that something will not get cleaned because I won't move the stuff.

Gross, right? But I can't deny it. Show me a shelf or a table with lots of small items sitting on it and I will show you a surface bearing an unhealthy quantity of dust.

I began this book with the assertion that an organized life supports an organized mind. This was what first drew me to *minimalism*, the lifestyle of living with less. Along the way, I learned that having less stuff didn't just sharpen my focus. It made the tedious work of doing my chores a lot easier.

As a kid, I remember my dad giving me a lecture about the half-hearted job I'd just done cleaning the house.

"Horizontal surface," he said as he pointed to a towel bar. "Horizontal surface." A beveled detail on a piece of furniture. "You have to go through and clean *every horizontal surface.*"

To this day, I still assess rooms and furniture based on their number of horizontal surfaces. I try to keep large horizontal surfaces as uninterrupted as possible to make them quick and easy to clean. Before adding an end table or other extra piece of furniture, I ask myself whether its utility makes it worth adding another horizontal surface. I love a clean house, but I don't love to clean.

Think of this as a pre-emptive form of Mini Habits. You're setting yourself up for chores that feel more like a Mini Habit than an all-day project. When I see a dusty surface, I'll pull out the duster and take care of it immediately — if this exercise can be done with *almost no effort.* I wipe down my kitchen counters every night — or at least the parts I can see without moving anything. The only way to facilitate this level of laziness is to reduce the number of individual objects laying around. In other words, to make the chore itself embarrassingly easy.

I use the word "laziness" in the most positive light possible here. We're not labeling ourselves (or our housemates!) as lazy people, but creating an environment that supports lazy cleaning. I categorize keeping a clean house as a basic adult skill we should all practice and attempt to master. It's good for your health, your self-esteem, and your social life. But I'm pretty sure we all have better, more important, more *fun* things to do than spend hours each week scrubbing and dusting. Remember the Agile Manifesto: maximize the amount of work *not done,* and make sure your routines are sustainable for the long term.

Remember *Rule #2: You Need a Container,* and all those baskets? Baskets aren't just a mind-and-clutter-clearing tool, they're a cleaning tool. I won't move a heap of shoes to vacuum the sand, leaves, and dirt from underneath. I will move a basket of shoes while I'm vacuuming. This makes all the difference in the world.

Give yourself permission to be lazy when it comes to cleaning. Look around your house and pay special attention to your horizontal surfaces. Do you have a lot of small items collected on your floors, tables, shelves, and kitchen counters? Contain them, put them in a cabinet with a door, or better yet, ask yourself if you really need them. Do you have a lot of small furniture pieces? Does your furniture have a lot of nooks, crannies, and bevels? Ask yourself how much you really love it or use it. When you view your home and the stuff in it through the lens of "I have to clean all of this," you begin to see things differently.

At the end of the day, your home and possessions are yet another commitment. You've already looked at your commitments to yourself and others. You've asked yourself which are worth the demands they make on your time and which you should consider letting go. Now it's time to examine your commitment to your stuff. Our stuff requires time and energy, too, even if it's just the few seconds we spend picking it up to vacuum underneath it. I've been known to get rid of items from my house for no reason other than I got tired of cleaning around them. Be ruthless with your time in all areas of your life. Don't let your stuff steal any more time than it deserves or keep you from having a clean, healthy home.

KEY TAKEAWAYS

- If you have to move something out of the way to clean a surface in your home, you're less likely to clean there.

- Keeping a clean home is important, but it's not worth spending a lot of your precious time.

- Contain, put away, or get rid of items that make cleaning inconvenient.

- Maximize the amount of work *not done*.

FEWER STEPS TO GET ANYWHERE

I called this book a quick-start guide, and I've tried to make it quick. Don't let that word fool you. Every chapter represents a major project for someone reading these words. Getting organized is hard work. Staying organized is no easier. It doesn't take long to tell you the basics, but you're in for a lifelong project.

That's why it's so important to reduce the size of your tasks, the amount of stuff you have to deal with, the number of commitments on your calendar. And the number of steps to get where you're going.

With everything you do, remember to keep it simple. Remove any step, any barrier, in every process you can. For people with ADHD, a seemingly trivial barrier can derail an entire process, sometimes permanently. You can't afford complications.

KEEP STUFF WHERE YOU USE IT

Remember how I bought a pair of scissors for each floor of my house because I realized no one would ever tackle a flight of stairs to put them away? Well, it works both ways. If I don't enjoy using something — toilet cleaner, for example — a flight of stairs provides the perfect excuse not to retrieve it.

For items your brain will always try to weasel out of using, shorten the distance between that thing and the place you must use it. This means I keep a toilet brush and toilet cleaner in each bathroom, not in a central storage area for cleaning supplies. I store refills for each soap dispenser under the sink. Each bathroom and the kitchen all have their own bottle of multi-purpose cleaner, a stockpile of rags, and a canister of disposable cleaning wipes. When any surfaces in these rooms need cleaning, I can address the problem quickly without leaving the room.

This might feel wasteful to you, or like you're creating extra clutter. Growing up, I remember our household cleaning supplies being stored in a few central locations. This allows you to own fewer individual bottles of stuff, but it also gives you the idea that you need to make a plan and gear up for even a minor cleaning task. If you're anything like me, you'll decide today is just not a convenient time for such a project.

If you're trying to convince other people in your household to help with chores, make it laughably easy for them. I keep a bottle of shower cleaner and a scouring pad in the shower's shampoo caddy. Anyone can clean the shower *during their daily bathing time* without gathering any supplies. While my husband is showering, I can lean in the door and ask him, "Can you clean the shower while you're in there?" This request is much harder to refuse than the one made while he's sitting on the couch.

Apply this not just to cleaning, but to any task you tend to avoid doing. When I'm working on my Weekly Review or emptying my inbox, I make sure I don't need to get up or leave the room for anything. If some of my tools or supplies are out of reach, I will avoid the tasks that require them. ADHD brains are fantastically adept at inventing reasons to avoid an undesirable task. While you'll never seal off all the excuses, you can eliminate the low-hanging fruit by keeping the tools for your chores within arm's reach.

SKIP THAT TRIP TO GOODWILL

I hope you'll finish this book feeling inspired to sort through your stuff and get rid of anything you no longer need or appreciate. Having inherited my grandmother's obsession with "waste not, want not," not to mention a healthy dose of concern for the environment,

I can't stand throwing anything away. And I don't need to. There are countless charities dedicated to getting our unwanted stuff into the hands of people who need it.

Packing up those unwanted items for donation is only half the battle for the declutterer with ADHD. Decluttering experts suggest several ways to make sure this stuff actually leaves your house: for example, keeping it in the car or dropping it off that very day, or collecting bags in your garage to take to Goodwill when you're done.

It's not that easy when you have ADHD. After my son's fourth birthday party, I shoved six pizza boxes into my car to drop off at the sanitation yard on my next errand. I do a lot of errands and the sanitation yard is a five-minute drive from home. The boxes sat in my car for *weeks*. As a teen, I once filled my entire trunk with books to donate to charity. They created a drag on my acceleration and gas mileage for several months. If I could forget about an entire room in my house, certainly I could not expect myself to attend to a bunch of junk I'd shoved into my car (or basement, or garage).

I've found one thing that works: whether you're throwing away or giving away, do it without leaving your home. Don't create another errand or another project to address the boxes or bags of unwanted items you've collected.

The best way to do this is via a charity pickup service like GreenDrop. Many organizations send postcards or other mailers to advertise their services. I've received them from the Lupus Foundation of America, the National Federation for the Blind, and the Military Order of the Purple Heart. If you live in a populated area, chances are you can find a charity pickup service to come right to your door.

These services require you to schedule a pickup on a designated day, which gives you the added benefit of an external deadline to gather all your stuff. On your pickup day, a truck will come through your neighborhood and collect the packed boxes from your front stoop. No remembering to drop stuff off or hiding it in the garage.

If you don't have access to a pickup service or you have an item they don't accept (like an old television), try Freecycle. A visit to www.freecycle.org will connect you to your local chapter, where you can post offers of specific items and coordinate with recipients to have them picked up. Social media networks like Nextdoor and Facebook frequently host freecycle or online yard sale groups as well.

Whatever you do — even if it's just texting a friend a picture of an item and asking, "This looks like your kind of thing, do you want it?" — prioritize decluttering streams that let you get rid of unwanted stuff without leaving your house. You will always be able to find reasons not to stop by the donation bins. It's harder to avoid scheduling a charity pickup when you can do it on the couch in your pajamas.

VALUE YOUR TIME, AND BEWARE OF CRAIGSLIST

When I declutter, I'm always tempted to sell unwanted stuff. The prospect of a few bucks in my pocket clouds my judgement. Sometimes I forget my goal: to simplify my life. To lower my stress and anxiety.

Money is great, but be careful about selling too much. Sometimes it costs more than the stuff is worth. The trick is to know when to sell and when to give away — and when your ADHD might tip the scales.

The temptation to make a few bucks grows especially strong with possessions that feel valuable or that were a significant investment when we acquired them. I encountered just such a scenario when I decluttered our video game collection. Even though our Guitar Hero equipment was outdated, I thought I could get $60 for it. I listed it on several local websites, and finally got a bite on Craigslist.

Because the box of Guitar Hero instruments had sat in our storage room for a few years, the buyer wanted to test everything before giving me cash. He asked if I might bring the equipment to him — an hour away.

I almost said yes. Then I stopped mid-text message and reminded myself: my time is valuable. I've already spent time texting with this guy and writing for-sale posts.

It's easy to hyperfocus on pieces of the decluttering process, especially when we think we can make an extra buck. My brain zeroed in on one goal — selling this stuff and getting the task out of my stack — and blocked out everything else. I almost forgot to stop and look at the big picture.

The big picture, as in I was considering spending two hours in the car to sell game controllers for $60. In many ways, my time is priceless. If I'm putting a number on writing alone, an hour is worth more than $60. The math didn't add up.

The Value of a Dollar

Of course, these scales will tip at a different point for each person or family. We all value a dollar (or 10) differently at various points in our lives. These guidelines keep me sane while I'm simplifying and paring down. Tweak them until they work for you.

- First, ask yourself how much you can get for the item. A quick search on Craigslist should give you an idea. Something you can sell for $500 is worth a lot more effort than a collection of $10-$20 items.

- Then, set a deadline to sell it. Commit to donating the item or giving it away if it hasn't sold within a few weeks.

- Set boundaries *before* you list something for sale. Examples from my life: I only communicate via text or email (no calls). I won't drive more than 10 minutes to meet someone. If plans to meet fall through, I may consider rescheduling once — but not after that. Most of all, I use my intuition. If someone feels difficult to schedule or communicate with, I remind myself I don't owe them anything and I move on.

Our time and energy are valuable. People with ADHD struggle to budget these resources and often shortchange our true priorities. As you can see from the list above, each item sold online represents a project. All the more reason to think twice before selling tchotchkes on the internet or elsewhere.

The reality is, ADHD makes the extra step — selling rather than tossing into a donation bin — more difficult. Accept that fact without judgement, then make choices that work for you. Sometimes the wisest choice is boxing it all up and scheduling a charity pickup, even if some items might be worth a little something.

Remember: Your goal is to get organized, not to walk away $172 richer than when you started. Keep an eye on your Why, and don't let lust for short-term reward get in the way of your long-term goals.

KEY TAKEAWAYS

- Once you identify items you want to get rid of, don't allow that to become another big project.

- Charity pick-up services like GreenDrop can collect boxes of unwanted items directly from your house, no extra errands required.

- Even if something is worth a few dollars, sometimes it makes more sense to donate it rather than waste time selling it.

THE DAILY GRIND: STAYING ORGANIZED FOR THE LONG HAUL

IN SUMMARY

Over the length of this book, we've talked about every step of the organizing process:

1. **Get to know yourself**: your brain, your personality, your values. Then...

2. **Accept reality**. Work *with* your brain and your ADHD, not against it. Never try to make yourself do something because you think you should. Be true to yourself and your Why. Before you try to organize everything...

3. **Contain it**. Contain your stuff, contain distraction and hyperfocus traps, contain all the information in your life. Contain your deadlines, obligations, appointments, and life events on a calendar. Above all, remember your brain should *never* serve as your container. The container needs to be external in order for your brain to...

4. **Establish a system that works *for you***. Identify a tool for managing your tasks and projects — a tool that feels right, like something you'll actually use. Then...

5. Grab that inbox and **work through it piece by piece**. If you're worried about how this system is going to lead you to an organized life...

6. **Lower the bar**. Progress happens step by tiny step. The only way to empty your inbox is by dealing with it one thing at a time. The only way to finish a project is by taking it one step at a time. Don't give up just because magic failed to happen on the first day. Work tirelessly to pare down your life so you have less to deal with in the first place. Accept small wins. Big wins are hard to repeat and sustain, anyway.

Perhaps most important is that you work with, not against, yourself. Those of us with ADHD have spent our entire lives fighting with ourselves. At 17, I wrote in my diary of my suspected ADHD: "I have to constantly stay a step ahead of this, I have to beat it, and sidestep it, and wrestle it to the ground, all to keep my head above the water." It took several years after this journal entry for me to collapse under the weight of the daily battle and seek treatment. This life — one that pitted me against my own brain every hour of every day — wasn't sustainable.

As you take small steps to a more organized life, know your mind. Know when your system won't (and shouldn't) look like everyone else's.

The more you accept your reality and work within it rather than trying to change it, the better you position yourself to create an organizing strategy that works for you. Remember: maximize the amount of work *not done*. Start where you are, not where you think you should be, and work from there.

A FEW LAST WORDS

Is your head spinning? I know I've only given you a brief tour of what it takes to organize your life. In truth, learning to get and stay organized is something you'll need to learn by doing, with plenty of mistakes along the way. I hope you'll come back to this book at various points in your journey and join our online community to share your progress and keep learning.

I've included links to *The ADHD Homestead* and other suggested reading at the end of this book. The books listed there are well worth the time you'll spend reading (or listening, if you prefer audiobooks). I owe much of this book, and my personal organizing success, to them.

If you take nothing else from this book, let it be this: keep looking for ways to merge your desired path with the path of least resistance. Remind yourself daily to let go of any shame you feel about your ADHD and how it has impacted your life. View every failure as a data point and nothing more. Each data point gives you a clue to the puzzle. This is how you maximize the amount of work and struggle *not done*. It's how you keep the machine of your life (and your brain) running smoothly.

Whatever you do, stop listing "try harder" as a possible solution to anything. Brute force, mental or physical, will only serve you in the short term — if you're lucky.

At the same time, don't think too much about the finish line. Or, more accurately, think about the finish line — your Why, the person you want to be and the life you want to have — but force the space between you and that perfect life out of your mind. If you've ever gone rappelling, or gotten yourself onto a ski slope that was steeper than you anticipated, maybe you know how it feels to spend too long staring at what lies before you. The enormity of it can paralyze you. One of my favorite pieces of ski slope signage simply read, "No easy way down." But once I'd gotten off the lift, down was the only way left to go.

There's no easy way to get where you're going. You may take a tumble and you may, at some point, question why you attempted such a thing. In skiing, this reflection sometimes comes after what we call a *yard sale*: where you land somewhere down the hill, with both skis and both poles scattered across the slope around you. If you're lucky, a friend skiing behind you will help collect your gear. If not, you must hike back up the hill, reattach your skis to your boots, and continue your progress with as much dignity as you can muster.

Real life has provided me with more such yard sales than any day on the slopes. I've learned there's really only one proper reaction to either: stand up, get my bearings, and summon the courage to laugh it off and keep going. The path may be long, but if you're willing to learn to do it right, fail repeatedly, and make slow and steady progress through the toughest parts, you'll make it in one piece.

I wish you the best on this journey.

SUGGESTED READING

Please stay in touch! Sign up for my email list at http://bit.ly/ADHDemails to get bonus tips, submit your own questions and feedback, and hear about future books and other projects.

You can follow my blog, *The ADHD Homestead*, at www.ADHDhomestead.net. I publish articles about the unexpected ways adult ADHD affects our lives and what we can do to build a peaceful home and family.

Below are a just a few of my favorite resources on ADHD, brains, and productivity.

WEBSITES & BLOGS

ADHD Roller Coaster
www.adhdrollercoaster.org
News and essays about adult ADHD from author and expert Gina Pera. Includes a wealth of guest posts and book excerpts.

A Dose of Healthy Distraction
www.adoseofhealthydistraction.com
A central hub for Liz Lewis' online community for women with ADHD. Friendly, honest, and supportive.

How to ADHD
www.howtoadhd.com
A central hub for ADHD education based on the YouTube channel *How to ADHD* by Jessica McCabe. Very friendly and informative.

BOOKS

Adult ADHD

Barkley, R. A. (2010).
    Taking charge of adult ADHD. New York, NY: The Guilford Press.
    A comprehensive guide to adult ADHD. Includes plenty of approachable scientific information blended with practical tips for improving your life.

Pera, G. (2008).

Is it you, me, or adult A.D.D.? Stopping the roller coaster when someone you love has attention deficit disorder. San Matteo, CA: 1201 Alarm Press.

Written for spouses or partners of adults with ADHD, but an eye-opener for anyone who wants to learn more about how ADHD affects home life and relationships.

Productivity

Allen, D. (2015).

Getting things done: The art of stress-free productivity. New York, NY: Penguin Books.

The definitive resource on personal productivity.

McGonigal, K. P. (2012).

The willpower instinct: How self-control works, why it matters, and what you can do to get more of it. New York, NY: Penguin Group.

A fascinating look at the brain's capacity to exert willpower in a variety of situations.

Rock, D. (2009).

Your brain at work: Strategies for overcoming distraction, regaining focus, and working smarter all day long. New York, NY: HarperCollins.

More productivity and communication advice through the lens of brain science. Uses a fictional story about a married couple to illustrate concepts.

REFERENCES

Agile Alliance, The. (2001). *Principles behind the Agile Manifesto*. Retrieved from http://agilemanifesto.org/iso/en/principles.html

ADDitude Editorial Board. (2018). *How ADHD impacts sex and marriage*. Retrieved from ADDitude: https://www.additudemag.com/adhd-marriage-statistics-personal-stories/

Allen, D. (2015). *Getting things done: The art of stress-free productivity*. New York, NY: Penguin Books.

Amen Clinics. (2017, November 30). Retrieved from https://www.amenclinics.com/healthy-vs-unhealthy/attention-deficit-disorder-addadhd/

Barkley, R. P. (2010). *Taking charge of adult ADHD*. New York, NY: The Guilford Press.

Carroll, R. (2017). *Bullet Journal - About*. Retrieved November 23, 2017, from Bullet Journal: http://bulletjournal.com/about/

Cheever, N. A. (2014). Out of sight is not out of mind: The impact of restricting wireless mobile device use on anxiety levels among low, moderate and high users. *Computers in Human Behavior*, 37, 290-297.

Dunn, R. B. (2002). Survey of research on learning styles. *California Journal of Science Education*, 75-98.

Feiler, B. (2013, February). *Agile programming — for your family* [Video file]. Retrieved from TED: https://www.ted.com/talks/bruce_feiler_agile_programming_for_your_family

Gerstel, N., & Gallagher, S. K. (1993). Kinkeeping and distress: Gender, recipients of care, and work-family conflict. *Journal of Marriage and the Family*, 598-608.

Guise, S. (2013). *Mini habits: Smaller habits, bigger results*. Amazon Digital Services.

Hardwick, C. (2014). *The nerdist way: How to reach the next level (in real life)*. Berkley.

Highsmith, J. (2001). Retrieved from History: The Agile Manifesto: http://agilemanifesto.org/history.html

Hinshaw, S. P., & Ellison, K. (2016). *ADHD: What everyone needs to know*. New York, NY: Oxford University Press.

Kellogg, R. T. (1989). *Cognitive tools and thinking performance: The case of word processors and writing*.

Kolberg, J., & Nadeau, K. (2002). *ADD-friendly ways to organize your life*. New York, NY: Brunner-Routledge.

Kondo, M. (2014). *The life-changing magic of tidying up*. Berkeley: Ten Speed Press.

Lewis, L. (2017, December 9). *I hated being a stay-at-home mom*. Retrieved from The Huffington Post: https://www.huffingtonpost.com/liz-lewis/i-hated-being-a-stay-at-home-mom_b_8683406.html

Mann, M. (2006, January 4). *Fresh start: The email DMZ*. Retrieved from 43 Folders: http://www.43folders.com/2006/01/04/email-dmz

McGonigal, K. P. (2012). *The willpower instinct: How self-control works, why it matters, and what you can do to get more of it*. New York, NY: Penguin Group.

Mueller, P. A., & Oppenheimer, D. M. (2014). The pen is mightier than the keyboard: Advantages of longhand over laptop note taking. *Psychological Science*, 1159-1168.

Nakamura, J., & Csikszentmihalyi, M. &. (2009). Flow theory and research. In *Oxford Handbook of Positive Psychology* (pp. 195-206). Oxford University Press.

Paul, J. (2015, May 4). *Book review: Healing ADD from the inside out*. Retrieved from The ADHD Homestead: http://adhdhomestead.net/book-review-daniel-amen-healing-add/

Paul, J. (2015, July 20). *What you need to know about ADHD, impulsivity, and self-harm*. Retrieved from The ADHD Homestead: http://adhdhomestead.net/adhd-impulsivity-and-self-harm/

Pennsylvania Higher Education Assistance Agency. (2017, November 30). Retrieved from EducationPlanner.org: http://www.educationplanner.org/students/self-assessments/learning-styles-styles.shtml

Pera, G. (2008). *Is it you, me, or adult A.D.D.? Stopping the roller coaster when someone you love has attention deficit disorder*. San Mateo, CA: 1201 Alarm Press.

Pera, G. (2015, February 23). *ADHD and sex: Post-orgasm irritability and jerkdom.* Retrieved from ADHD roller coaster: News and essays about adult ADHD: https://adhdrollercoaster.org/adhd-news-and-research/adhd-post-sex-irritability-jerkiness/

Pera, G. (2016, June 25). *What traits attracted you to your ADHD partner?* Retrieved from ADHD Rollercoaster: https://adhdrollercoaster.org/adhd-and-relationships/what-traits-attracted-you-to-each-other/

Rosenthal, C. J. (1985). Kinkeeping in the familial division of labor. *Journal of Marriage and the Family*, 965-974.

Rubin, G. (2015). *Better than before: Mastering the habits of our everyday lives.* New York, NY: Crown Publishers.

Vedantam, S. (Host). (2017, October 30). Check yourself [Audio podcast episode]. In *Hidden Brain*. Washington, DC: National Public Radio. Retrieved from https://www.npr.org/templates/transcript/transcript.php?storyId=560014313

Widrich, L. (2017, December 11). *Why we have our best ideas in the shower: The science of creativity.* Retrieved from Buffer Social: https://blog.bufferapp.com/why-we-have-our-best-ideas-in-the-shower-the-science-of-creativity

TABLE OF FIGURES